The Lean Manager's Playbook

Derrick Mains

Contents

Introduction

Top-line revenue does not translate to bottom-line profits.

Profit is a deliberate by-product of a well-run business. Most businesses focus on growth, sales and scale, and forget that business is both offensive and defensive. Thus, they lose far more profit than they capture.

Although the setting for this book is in a production factory, the lessons are universal. I write it for those of you who want more profits; who want to better understand why your business is growing, but profits are shrinking; why the mysterious "economies of scale" have not come into effect in your business.

This book can help, if you let it.

Derrick

Chapter 1

The Factory

"Steve, can I see you here in my office?"

"Sure, Susan, I'll be right up."

Susan hung up the phone and awaited Steve's arrival to her office while thinking to herself,
"This can't be right—sales are through the roof, and yet somehow we are less profitable? I need answers."

Steve arrived after a few moments and Susan spoke.

"Steve, take a seat. I think you need to have accounting rerun these Q2 numbers. Sales are up—way up—and this is our third quarter in a row with record revenues, yet somehow our profits are down significantly over last year. Q1 was off and we thought it was because of some discounting our sales people did to gain some new accounts. But now Q2 is worse!"

Steve spoke cautiously. "Susan, the numbers are correct. I reran them myself. Our executive focus and goals have been on driving more revenue, and better recruiting and training for our people. That gamble didn't work out. In the end, Ben's prediction was accurate. The improvement in revenue did nothing to the bottom line and the focus on hiring better labor ended up just costing us more. Worse, the overtime the production floor now requires in meeting the increased demand is at a higher wage than we ever experienced before. A great job market means, even without the OT, we would pay more. OT just exacerbates the issue."

"What about the economies of scale we anticipated? What about our volume increase? Have we not negotiated better costs because of our increased volume?"

"On the contrary, Susan. Raising wages affected all of our vendors, particularly the ones that rely upon unskilled labor. The minimum wage increase hit them hard, so their costs went up. If anything, our increase in volume discounts didn't even offset their price increases across the board.

Worse the consequences of these new tariffs haven't even affected us yet."

"So all this focus on better people and more sales did nothing?" Susan said in a concerned voice.

"It did something, just not the something we had hoped. Unfortunately, it deteriorated our margins and dried up our profits."

"Steve, what do we need to do here? My call with the Board is next Friday and I can't present these numbers without a plan. Every Board member will ask about how we will handle the new tariffs: will we pass the costs on to customers, or absorb the cost and hope we can wait it out and force our competitors either out of the market or out of business? That conversation is tough enough, but coupled with this it won't be pretty.

"7% EBITDA has always been our target and we have never failed to meet it, not even in the recession. Q1 was 4.5%. Now these Q2 numbers are 3.9%! At 7%, absorbing the tariff was risky; at 4% it's impossible. Steve, have you sent these numbers to the bank yet?"

"Not yet, Susan, but they require them by next Friday in order to keep our Credit Line open. I don't anticipate that a two-quarter blip will cause us to lose Line of Credit access, but certainly this will trigger a review and, if we don't turn this around quick, well then…"

" 'Well then' is not going to happen. We need to act now!" Susan retorted.

"Steve, contact Ben and see if he can meet us tomorrow morning for breakfast."

Steven nodded in acknowledgment and headed downstairs. He entered his office and slumped back into his office chair. "How did we get in this mess? All these years of consistent profit and, in less than 6 months, it is nearly gone. And the next 6 months? I don't even want to think about it. We need help, now. I better call Ben right now. No, better yet, I'll head down to the diner and see if he is in."

· · · · · ● ● ● ● ● ● · · · · · ·

"Good morning!" "Welcome!" "Take a seat where ever you like!" A chorus of voices called out before the bells hanging from the door had a chance to stop resonating.

Steve looked in the corner where Ben was usually found, but instead found the booth chock full of business people frantically discussing some innovation while filling their mouths with pie and hot coffee.

"Excuse me, miss. Do you know Ben, the guy that is usually in this booth this time of day?"

"Of course. But he hasn't been here in a few weeks. Not sure if you heard, but The Diner is going mainstream. We opened a second location three months ago and a third location two weeks back, over on 3rd and Winchester. Ben has been 'officing' there," the waitress said while holding up her fingers in air quotes, "ever since the grand opening. He is quite close with Sophia, our General Manager and head of franchising, and has been over there lending a set of eyes to the operation. I'm sure you can catch him over there—booth in the same front corner, overlooking the intersection."

"Thanksforthehelp,umm…"Stevelookedatthenametag on the helpful waitress. "…Anna. Appreciate the help."

Steve sprinted out the door like a man on a mission. After a quick Lyft and twelve blocks later, he was met with a repeat of the angelic chorus he had just heard at the original location. "Good morning!" "Welcome!" "Take a seat where ever you like!"

Steve made a b-line to the front corner booth and made eye contact with Ben as he approached.

"Steve, fancy meeting you here! How're things down at the factory?"

"Just awful, Ben—awful! OK if I join you?"

"Sure, Steve, what can I help with?" Ben inquired.

"Ben, we need you to come down to the factory and give us some advice. We are crushing our goals for the year, but… well…"

Ben interrupted, "The goals have crushed you. Instead of an increase in profits, profits are falling and with the new tariffs on the horizon you'll likely be in a desperate situation by end of year."

"Yeah, Ben, that's it. Just like you predicted. All this focus on sales, driving revenue, more customers, and more product lines has all added up to more revenue and fewer profits."

"How bad is it?" asked Ben.

"Bad enough that Susan sent me down here to see if you can meet for breakfast tomorrow."

"I see." Ben nodded. "Tell you what; let's skip breakfast and I'll meet you at your first Walkabout of the morning. You and Susan do it together, and I'll join. What time do you do your morning routine?"

"Ben, to be honest we don't really do the routine. We read your <u>Frontline Manager's Playbook</u> and we both really enjoyed it. But I will admit we never really took action. Sometimes we do an all shop meeting, which is like a Huddle, and I know we do more walkabouts than we ever did before—but I wouldn't say we drank the Kool-Aid. Reality is the other consultants we worked with thought those things were a waste of effort. Instead, they wanted us to focus on our vision and mission, our values, and getting the executive team out of the building to think about and work through our strategic objectives. The efficiency tools in your book never took hold."

"How'd that work out for you, Steve?"

"In hindsight, Ben, awful. The idea of more revenue, new products, and what our 3-, 5-, and 10-year plans had enthralled us, and we relied upon the 'economies of scale' to make it all work. In the end, well, it might be our undoing."

"Steve, it's not that those things are bad; it's that those things always come second to systems and processes. Do you remember my analogy of the fish bowl from when we first met?"

Steve nodded his head yes.

"Well, let me remind you anyway." Ben continued.

"Imagine you had a fishbowl and, each day, you noticed small leaks in the bowl were causing the water level to drop.

"Would you blame the fish?

"Would you just keep adding more water?

"Or, would you repair the leaks in the bowl?

"Now, let's consider that the fish are your employees, the water represents your revenues, and the cracks are all the lost profit that occurs from ill-defined or ineffective processes.

"Just as a fishbowl with cracks won't hold water, a business that is leaking out profits from poor process cannot stay profitable."

Steve nodded again in agreement as a waiter buzzed over to the table with a hot pot of coffee and looked at Steve for acknowledgement.

"Coffee?" The waiter inquired. Steve slid his cup toward the waiter as Ben continued.

"While repairing the fishbowl seems obvious, modern management says, 'If we just had more revenue, aka water, or better trained people, aka fish, everything will work itself out.'

"The truth of the matter is that adding more revenues or offering more training to your people doesn't fix ineffective processes that cause waste to occur in your business.

"Waste is the nemesis to profits.

"More water and more training do not solve the problem of the fishbowl. If anything, they make it worse."

"I remember, Ben. Can you help us?"

"Steve, what time does your first shift start working?"

"7 a.m."

"Great. I will see you at 6:30 a.m. for some preparation before your 6:45 morning Huddle and to make sure you and Susan are there.

But I'd like to come by at 1:30 today for a Walkabout with just you two. Does that work as well?"

"Yes, Ben, I'll be there for sure and will try to get Susan. Worst case, I'll make sure Susan is present tomorrow morning."

Chapter 2
The Enemies of EBITDA

"Susan, Steve, good to see you again. How're sales?" Ben asked.

Susan spoke up. "Sales are great! But, Ben, I need to apologize to you. We were a bit flippant with your advice last year. We went with the tried-and-true idea of more sales and better people. It all sounded good: sell, sell, sell, hire the best, get the right people in the right seats and let them loose to do what they do but, in the end, it didn't work out. We pay more now for less productivity and the increase in revenue had a negative effect on our profits. Honestly, we aren't totally sure we have a handle on all the reasons we are trending down. But the line is clear.

"Not sure if Steve told you, but I have a Board meeting next Friday and I need a plan—something that is actionable, something that will improve the numbers next quarter, even while knowing that these damn tariffs will put a squeeze on us. Ben, we need your help and your advice on how to act quickly and whip this place into shape."

"Susan, I can help, but it will require work on you and your teams' part. This will require a change in the way you think, as well as the actions you do daily, and it will challenge you and your level of comfort every day.

But if you are up for the challenge, we can whip this thing into shape and not only present a plan, but show marked improvement between now and the Board meeting. Deal?"

"Deal," said Susan. "Where do we start?"

"I heard from Steve that the Huddle and Walkabouts aren't happening consistently. Getting out onto the floor, seeing the work, and hearing from your people is critical to finding the leaks and correcting the ship. Let's go for a Walkabout and then let's get the team together 15 minutes before the shift starts tomorrow for a launch meeting. I will take the lead in explaining the Huddle concept and schedule."

"I trust you, Ben, how can I not; you predicted this would happen."

"Susan, do you remember the concept of the Huddles."

"Yes." Susan wrinkled her face a bit. "But our challenge was it just didn't work.

"Everyone attended, but we didn't get a lot of feedback. Shift managers gave out job assignments and asked people what they were working on. Pretty quickly things got out of hand; people complaining about things, job conditions, other people, management. Stories rattled on for minute after minute with no real intention or conclusion. Ben, the Huddles just didn't work for us. They were a distraction."

"Susan, first and foremost I am not really sure what job assignments have to do with a Huddle or how someone could rattle on or voice any complaint. The scripted nature of the Huddle prevents that from happening, and the time restrictions and limitations ensure it."

The Huddle is a standup meeting where people share their successes and barriers. No job assignments— just a brief meeting, a few minutes long, to make sure everyone is accountable. From what you just explained, it sounded like management did the talking and the employees did the ignoring."

Susan's head bobbed in agreement. "Ignoring is right! It seemed most of the people were day dreaming. We asked them to provide details, but no one really did. And, if they did, it was usually a dissertation about poor materials, work conditions, or management."

"And that, folks, is why Huddles fail," Ben said. "You never did it with any sort of cadence or rhythm. The Huddle is important; it does two things. First, it creates a place where people commit to daily accomplishments. Second, it gives managers marching orders on the real barriers that are stopping people from obtaining their goals.

"The Huddle might seem tedious, but if it is truly short and on point, it will make a world of difference to your people and your profits. Think about Huddles in sports; they are brief. They tell the players the plays, and the players have a chance to give quick feedback on where there are holes and gaps. The Huddle is an essential part of the game. Tomorrow, I'll get the team started and set you up for success. For now, let's walk."

Steve, Susan, and Ben all headed toward the production floor. As they walked, Tia blew past them all like a woman on a mission, starting down at her iPad and not even seeing the team assembled.

"Tia," Steve called out to get Tia's attention. "I want to introduce you to Ben. Ben is helping us find waste here in The Factory and will provide us some tools to make our lives easier."

"Ben, it's very nice to meet you," Tia replied. "One of my high school friends and college roommate, Sophia, speaks very highly of you."

"That is very kind of her and it's nice to meet you. What's your role here at The Factory?"

Tia approached the topic a bit tentatively, which made Ben wonder. Tia replied, "Well, I do the scheduling, inventory, production; everything beyond that door there." Tia pointed to the factory doors."

"Just the person we were looking for," Ben chuckled. "Would you like to join us on our Walkabout?"

Without missing a beat, Ben continued walking toward the floor, ushering all three of them with a motion of his arm. Although Tia was in the middle of something, she knew that if Susan and Steve were paying attention, she should, too.

Ben entered the facility, stopped dead in his tracks, and spent a full minute in silence taking inventory of what was happening.

"Did you see that, folks?" asked Ben.

"Sorry, no, what did you notice, Ben?" Susan replied.

Ben continued. "The moment we walked out on the floor, the whole atmosphere changed. This operator over here to our left raised his hands above his head like he was stretching, and within a minute, other workers all over the floor did the same thing. Do you find that odd Steve?"

"Not sure, Ben. What are you thinking just happened?" Steve questioned.

"Oh, I am not thinking anything, I'm just observing. The instant management appeared on this floor, the whole dynamic changed. Look around; the banter among employees has stopped, people look busier, those who were walking around aimlessly now have brooms or inventory in hand. Watch for a moment. Eyes are on you and the reason is simple; the employees see you so infrequently that they have their own alert system to let others know when you are out here. Steve, Susan, be honest with me—when is the last time either of you walked out on this floor for a reason other than to check on an order status, or as the result of some proverbial fire? Last week? Last month? Last quarter?"

"I don't know, Ben, I can't recall the last time I just walked out here to see what was happening," Susan said over the hum of the machines. "But that is why we have Tia as our eyes and ears."

Steve shrugged his shoulders, not able to recall any instance himself.

Ben continued. "Your labor upgrade isn't working because people only respect what you inspect. If you fail to inspect, they will never respect the work.

"Tia is here, yes. But, Tia, do you spend any time just inspecting, or is your job to make sure things get done?"

Tia felt really uncomfortable with the line of questioning, but after seeing the way Ben was communicating with Susan and Steve and how they were listening, she knew she shouldn't sugar-coat it.

"Ben, I'll be honest, I am trying to keep the wheels moving. For the most part I can walk this whole place blindfolded. Most of the steps I take every day are checking on the status of orders, moving the schedule, scheduling the trucks, and making sure we have enough materials to complete orders."

"Thanks for your honesty, Tia. Susan, Steve, it is impossible for Tia to be the eyes and ears of the organization if she is primarily the hands. I can certainly help in giving Tia some tools to find the root cause of issues. But you have to support her by helping sniff out where waste is occurring.

"Oh, and Tia, when I say waste, I am not just talking about garbage. Waste is anything that is not adding value to the customer. Over the next couple weeks, you and I will spend a lot of time refining your ability to see waste, and Steve and Susan will be a part of that as well. So, the three of you can work as a team to resolve the issues you have here on the floor.

"Back to our Walkabout. Steve, Susan, you can't understand why the economies of scale didn't kick in? The economies of scale aren't magic; they are a deliberate outcome of a refined process, one that can handle more capacity.

"You aren't managing this business. You are managing numbers, emails, and invoices but the business is on auto-pilot and your auto-pilot isn't working."

Tia squirmed. Both Susan and Steve shook their heads. It was apparent the business was in trouble for a lack of management, not a lack of sales.

As the three proceeded on their Walkabout, Ben picked up things, smelled them, weighed them with his hand, held them up, turned them around, and checked every angle. Ben spend half his time looking in the trash bins, pulling out unfinished and abandoned product, and asking questions.

Each time, as the group of managers walked away, Tia noticed something happening behind them. As soon as the group moved on, the people in that area immediately went over to look at whatever Ben inspected; they asked questions of each other and scrutinized everything Ben had looked at.

Ben stopped at one of the stations and took a peek into the garbage bin located right beside the operator. "Hi, my name is Ben, what's yours?" Ben hollered over the hum of a big cutting machine running now at full speed.

"Gianni," the operator hollered back.

"Quick question for you, Gianni. Any reason all these products are in the trash bin? Are these mistakes?"

"No, not mistakes—just extras."

"Extras?" Ben asked in an inquisitive tone.

"Yeah," Gianni continued. "See, the operator on the line before me makes extras. That's the way we do it here just in case the counts were wrong or if I miss-cut something."

Ben wrinkled his forehead and inquired again, "I see. And do you make a lot of bad cuts with this machine?"

Gianni laughed, "Hardly ever, Ben. The computer on this machine makes sure every cut is perfect."

Ben asked, both puzzled and amused, "Hmm... so the overruns are in case we are short on an order then?"

"Yup," Gianni continued, "exactly. Sometimes, for some reason or another, we might need to make 3-5% more to fulfill the order. Maybe one product doesn't meet the QA standard, like when the material had a defect. It happens."

"I see," said Ben. "So, the 3-5% is necessary?"

Gianni shrugged as the cutter blade sliced through a huge stack of printed material with a mechanical thump.

Ben reached into the trash bin and took out every item that was an overrun for that particular order.

"Gianni, how many items did you need for this order?"

"250," Gianni yelled out over the machine cycling for its next cut.

Ben turned to Susan and Steve. "So then, how many overruns would be acceptable?

Steve spoke up. "At a 5% overrun, thirteen at the most."

Tia took a step back and clicked the unlock button on her iPad to take notes.

Ben began to count out loud as he tallied the pieces. "2, 4, 6, … 18, 24, 40. Forty pieces were overrun. You want to check my count, Steve?"

Steve's shoulders drooped. "No, Ben, I'm sure it's correct."

Ben continued. "Thirteen at the high end is acceptable— but we just counted forty. Didn't you say your margins have been shrinking?"

Both Steve and Susan nodded.

"Could this contribute to that?" Ben spoke again before the two could answer. "Of course, it could and does. I'd even question the need for 5%. What we need to know is, what's the standard deviation. Is it 3%? 2%? Less? And, if the material is the problem, are we getting credit from the vendor for defects? Can we find better material? A better supplier? Is one lot better than another? Since your Cost of Goods is rising, waste is more expensive today than it was a year ago."

Tia jotted in on her iPad the unfamiliar phrase she just heard, "Cost of Goods."

"We can see here that the only feedback loop to tell us there is a problem is right here in the trash bin. And the only one here with the ability and authority to get to the bottom of this is management.

Ben and Susan listened intently, and Tia slumped a bit. She was concerned that this was her fault.

Ben continued. "This handful of overruns is 100% lost profit. If you cut these from 40 to 20, you would recover 50% of the losses here, get it to target, and realize nearly 70% reduction in lost profit on these products. Really dig in and you might find there is no need for lost profit at all. These are the things management needs to focus on."

Nods came again from both the Executives.

Ben turned to Tia. "Tia, how much to you know about the term 'EBITDA'?"

Tia blushed, feeling she should know the answer.

Ben piped back in. "So, not enough, is the answer?"

Tia smiled nervously.

"Tia," Ben stepped closer to Tia to make sure she heard him over the noise, "EBITDA is profit before some other uncontrollable expenses, such as taxes. When we are talking about waste, we are referring to the things that take away from that number. I call them The Enemies of EBITDA and there are eight really distinct ones you can find in every business out there. They are really visible in an operation like this, but even software companies have every single one of them, just in a different light. The way to improve profits is to wage all-out war constantly on these things.

Ben looked back to Steve and Susan, and motioned to Tia to write a note in her iPad. "Do you both remember the TIM WOODS acrostic from the session I did with you last year?"

Susan and Steve both looked as if trying to remember.

"Transportation, Inventory, Motion..." Steve began before stalling out.

Susan jumped in, "Waiting, Over-production, Over-processing, Defects, and, umm..."

"Skills!" Steve piped back in.

"Glad to hear you remember them. Tia, did you get those?" Tia nodded. Ben continued, "We will focus extensively on these over the next two weeks. Anyone want to guess what we just found with Gianni?"

"Over-production?" Steve asked, unsure if that was the correct answer.

Susan replied, "So, I thought that was Over-processing."

"Well, you are both correct," Ben said gleefully. "Tia, what about you?"

"Ben, I thought it was an inventory problem."

Ben dug deeper. "Why?"

"Well," Tia continued, "those materials in the garbage were once inventory—inventory I bought, we stocked, and we pulled to feed the machines. It took up space, and our time and effort to move that material around; now we have to move it to the garbage. For me, I saw what affected me and how it affects me. More effort, more overtime."

"Bingo!" Ben hollered out, loud enough that two workers in the vicinity both jumped. "When it comes to waste, the general rule is that they all tend to be connected somehow. The over processing that Susan, as CEO, saw was the extra steps in handling the material after we don't use it. Steve, as the CFO, saw more how that waste was product no one pays for. Tia saw the amount of work it takes to order and move the inventory, and the physical waste.

"This is why it is really, really important for you all to be part of the process. You each have unique perspectives based upon what you see and do on a daily basis."

Ben motioned to them both that it was time to make their way to the door and back into the front offices.

As they entered the hallway between the offices and the production floor, both Susan and Steve looked frustrated.

Ben realized their frustration and assured them. "Look you two, this is not uncommon. Don't beat yourselves up. Just look at what we discovered in only a few minutes. Little things like that add up, quick."

Ben motioned back to the production floor. "First, your team works at a different pace and with a different attention to detail when you are physically present versus physically absent.

"Second, no one here is paying any attention to the bottom line. Sure, you are watching expenses and cutting costs where you can, but the item like we just found is a monster that eats profits for breakfast. Those overruns are the enemy and, if you were smart, you would focus on them and take action like you would if your building was on fire. It should be a top priority. But, to truly resolve it, you need to use the 5 Why's.

"Are you familiar with the 5 Why's technique?" Ben looked to both Susan and Steve for acknowledgement. Tia had never heard the saying before and unlocked her iPad to take notes.

Susan spoke, "I believe I remember that from management school—keep asking why to discover the root cause of an issue."

"Exactly!" Ben said. "Refuse to solve the issues until you know what caused the issue. Keep asking why over and over until you discover why this happened in the first place. Then resolve that root cause, create an error-proofed process, and develop the systems and tracking so that the situation can never occur again. If it happens again, return to the process, ask why again, and don't stop. Keep digging.

"Let's run through it with those overruns. Why are you losing money?"

Susan answered, "Because of the overruns."

"And why are their overruns?" Ben pointed back to Susan.

"Because either our counting is sloppy or we haven't properly trained our people on the standard."

"And why haven't we properly trained our people, to be precise?" Ben pointed again at Susan.

"Because we don't have a Standard procedure and expectation for what is acceptable."

"Why not?" Ben looked again to Susan.

"Well, honestly, I am not sure we even know what the Standard should be, so how can we train on it?"

Ben let that sink in a for moment, allowing Tia to finish up her note-taking, then he spoke up.

"So, what is the course of action, Susan?"

Tia reached down and turned on the recorder on the iPad; she didn't want to miss this.

Susan replied, "To determine an acceptable Standard for overruns, then visit with the vendor to understand why we are getting defective material and resolve the problem with them, then publish a procedure and acceptable measurement for what we expect of the operators."

"Yes," Ben exclaimed. "Then, as part of the daily Walkabouts, you inspect that trash bin and ask questions of yourself. Is this an acceptable amount? Is the number fluctuating? And if you find something, you start again with Why. But there is another critical step that is easy to miss. First let me ask you a question—do you know of Elon Musk and Tesla?"

Steve immediately spoke up with some excitement. "Know about them? I own one and so does my wife, and we have been buying their stock for years."

"Team, I have an assignment for you. This evening I will send you a quote from Elon Musk, then tomorrow let's discuss it. Sound good?"

All of them nodded in agreement.

"We'll get started tomorrow and I will see you 6:45 a.m.!"

·····•••●●••·····

Later that evening, Ben sent the following email.

Susan, Steve, Tia,

Good start today. I think you saw, like I did, that the first solution is right there on the shop floor. A good playbook, a solid cadence, and some awareness of the problems is the cure.

The assignment I have for you tonight is as follows:

Read this story about Elon Musk and his approach to a high number of injuries at his factory and think of how that incorporated into the 5-Why's Process, and how different it is from your current style of management.

In an email to all employees Musk wrote:

> *"No words can express how much I care about your safety and wellbeing. It breaks my heart when someone is injured building cars and trying their best to make Tesla successful.*
>
> *Going forward, I've asked that every injury be reported directly to me, without exception. I'm meeting with the safety team every week and would like to meet every injured person as*

soon as they are well, so that I can understand from them exactly what we need to do to make it better. I will then go down to the production line and perform the same task that they perform.

This is what all managers at Tesla should do as a matter of course. At Tesla, we lead from the front line, not from some safe and comfortable ivory tower. Managers must always put their team's safety above their own."

Read this a couple times. Let it soak in, then read it again and think of how that approach differs from the management style you are used to.

See you at 6:45 tomorrow morning for a team meeting/ Huddle.

Ben

Chapter 3
Why

"Good morning, team." Ben spoke loudly and with authority as he stood before the 50 or so employees of the factory. "My name is Ben, and I am working with the team here at the factory to help improve efficiency and implement some updated processes and systems.

"I've done this many times before, and I want to first tell you that this is not about cutting jobs. On the contrary, it is about making your jobs easier, more efficient, and giving you more time to be the experts on what we do here.

"Let me ask you a question: How many of you have ever felt overwhelmed or exhausted when you leave here for the day?"

A sea of hands went up.

"We are going to stop that. But, to do it, we need your help. We'll admit to you right now that as leaders we managed you, but we didn't lead you towards greater goals and accomplishments. That changes today and we are going to try to do this better, to do it differently. But I can tell you we will still fail. It will take time. This is not an overnight transformation—but you will see changes here today. That is for sure.

"What I need from you is help and guidance as we implement those changes. We are not changing things just to change them; our intent is to make this business better today than it was yesterday and better tomorrow than it is today. To do that, we have to try new things. It might mean moving equipment, changing the way we schedule work, or maybe even to stop doing something we are used to.

"A very wise person once said the seven most expensive words in business are, 'We have always done it that way.' We are going to change that, too—but we are going to do it with you. Some changes might be immediate and uncomfortable, but every change we make we will give you the opportunity to help us determine if it improves the business and your work in it.

"Sometimes, that might mean we pull a group aside to get your input. Other times, it might mean we make a change based on some data we are seeing, then ask you afterward how things felt, how they improved, or what new challenges those created.

"Does that sound fair to you?"

The majority of heads nodded as if they were awakening from some sort of slumber. In all their tenure at the factory, none of them were every asked to provide input or ideas; just do the work and keep quiet. The idea of participating in the changes excited some and terrified others.

"OK, then starting tomorrow we will have a daily Huddle starting promptly at 6:45 a.m. It is up to each one of you to bring a few things.

Each day, I would like you to come to the meeting with an accomplishment from the previous day—something you are proud of and might be willing to share.

Next, bring me a barrier that prohibits you from hitting our goals. I am not looking for big ideas, but simple, easy things we could do today that will make our jobs easier and get more, quality products out to the customers that love and depend on us.

We will start these Huddles as a team, but over time we will transition to these being by department.

"That's it. It's 'show and tell' every morning. See you all tomorrow at 6:45 a.m. sharp."

As the employees headed out to the floor and back into the office to start the day, Steve, Tia, and Susan waited behind.

"That seem to go over relatively well," said Steve. "There seemed to be an optimistic look about the crew. What did you think Susan?"

"Yeah, I would agree. The people did look like they paid attention and we got a lot of head nods. That's good, right?"

"It's a start," Ben said. "Tia, what did you think?"

"Ben, I am not sure. I need to get out and hcar the feedback. One thing you all probably didn't understand is that this is the first time, other than the company holiday party, that all of us in the back have been in the same room as Steve and Susan. I know people came to the meeting this morning concerned. An all-hands meeting is rarely a positive thing. I think your tone, Ben, and the way you explained things calmed everyone a little, but by the number of text messages I got last night, I can tell you this meeting was very different from the rumor mill."

"Good point, Tia! That is why the next few days are so important. If we want people to change, we have to change their behaviors and, to help us, we have to change what they see. This is the first step in that. Steve, I have another step you and I talk can about separately. For now, let's talk about the Elon Musk quote. What did you think?"

Susan spoke first. "It was both enlightening and terrifying. To be honest, I was taught that managers are the brains and workers are the brawn. Musk seems to think it's impossible to lead or improve something without doing it. I don't know how I feel about that. But I can see his point, and can draw the correlation between finding a problem and using the 5-Why's, if my goal is to get to the root of the problem and fix it. Data analysis and a change in policy won't always do it. Asking Why will tell me what needs to change, but not always the reality of how to do it. My Why's aren't complete until I get my hands in the process."

Steve jumped in, "I read that quote a few times last night, and before bed I shared it with my wife. Not sure if you know this but she is the head chef over at

Emanuel's on 11th Ave and Broadway."

"Love that place, best club sandwich I ever had!" Ben said.

"Right! That's the place. So, I read the quote to my wife last night and her interpretation was dead-on. She said she liked the quote because it reminded her of what top chefs do. The chef makes the recipe, cooks the dish, tastes it, smells it, touches it, thinks about the flavor profile, what the customer might think, thinks of ways to improve it, and then she repeats the process until she feels the dish is ready. Then, and only then, does she teach her cooks, sous-chefs, and kitchen staff the techniques and processes to prepare the dish. On a busy night, the chef is really just managing the kitchen; walking around, tasting things, making sure the dishes are consistent, and the flow of plates from the kitchen to the tables are symmetrical. No one wants one person to get their meal while everyone waits. She then visits tables and get their feedback on the new dish. If she is smart, she asks for candid feedback about the entire experience and will even ask customers who received that dish a few specific questions about it. What ingredient stood out? Did you like the presentation? The chef isn't performing a survey, but rather looking in the eyes of the customer and seeing the truth of how the dish performed.

"After my wife finished, I laid awake thinking about how we might run this place more like a chef; not just giving the recipe to the workers, but actually being a part of perfecting the process of that recipe until we have a standard for producing that product, then managing to the standard and making sure everyone stays compliant."

"Great perspectives on that," Ben said. "In your instance, you should think more about how you become a part of that process early on. But also, when you are trying to determine a root cause, before and after you make a change, you need to come down here to the front line and perform the task."

"Many times, we as leaders send a memo or an email or we post something on the bulletin board, and we believe our job is done. But business is about execution. Ideas are a dime a dozen; people who can execute on them are rare.

"Tia?" Ben turned to Tia for her response.

"Ben, for the most part the whole concept was so foreign to me that I just couldn't get over how nice of a guy Elon must be," Tia chuckled and continued. "I understood what he was saying, but it seemed to me that he would have bigger issues to deal with. Can't his team handle things like this?"

Ben replied, "Tia, great point and one that most management books would tell you is textbook. But what is the message Elon sends to his people, to his shareholders, to his customers by doing it his way?"

All three nodded as if pondering the question.

Ben continued. "He is saying something very profound about his business. Tesla is a company of doers. They don't just identify problems and delegate them to people to try to fix. No, they roll up their sleeves and do it themselves. They see problems as something they can use to better the company and they have an approach to execution that requires them to get hands-on."

Motioning to Susan and Steve, Ben continued. "As you both know, I love tools. I believe every leader should have a toolbox full of tried-and-true methods they can call upon in every situation. You are familiar with The Walkabout and The Huddle. So, let me take a second here and explain to Tia.

"Tia, the huddle is what we are starting tomorrow. It's a brief meeting where everyone stands and shares. I rarely run Huddles with this many people; I prefer 10-12 people at the most. But for now, let's set the tone. Let's show the team that management is onboard, then we can departmentalize.

"The Walkabout is what we did yesterday. Walking around and paying attention to the flow of the business with no judgement, no correction; just to understand what is happening and see what seems out of place.

"Susan explained the 5 Why's, which is an essential tool to discover why things are happening. And what we just spoke about with Elon Musk is something I call The DIY—the Do-It-Yourself. To truly understand the root of a problem, you must insert yourself in the system or process where the problem is occurring and perform the task yourself.

"I am not saying you need to go and work that job all day, but you should have your hand in the process at some point to see how your improvement worked.

"Susan, do you have a whiteboard I can use?"

"Sure, Ben." Susan pointed towards a conference room. "We can use this."

Ben continued by writing the steps on the board. "What you must do is:"

1. *Identify the root cause.*
2. *Create a list of solutions.*
3. *Select a relevant solution from your list.*
4. *Perform the process yourself using that solution.*
5. *Measure the improvement if any.*
6. *Revisit the problem area and do it yourself again to confirm it resolves the problem. If not, return to step 1.*

As a rule, the time involved in physically working the process is likely 15-30 minutes—the rest is cerebral.

"When you do this, remember to act the way you do on a Walkabout. Don't get upset, don't correct people.

Observe, be respectful, and ask questions.

"Does all that make sense?"

Both Susan and Steve nodded enthusiastically, while Tia snapped a picture of the whiteboard with her iPad.

Susan spoke. "It reminds me, Ben, of why people say senior management is in an ivory tower, disconnected from the actual business. There is a lot of truth to that."

"Yes, there is," Ben replied. "There certainly is. Well then, Susan and Steve, I will let you get back to business, and Tia and I will spend some time together.

Chapter 4

Inventory and Over Processing

"Tia, tell me a little about your role," Ben inquired.

"Mostly, I handle all the back-of-the-house business; ordering, inventory, scheduling and logistics. It's a lot of work. I get her at 6 a.m. each day and usually never leave before 4 p.m. The money is good, but the experience is priceless. I am only 26 and feel like I, and my friend Sophia, are way ahead of our peers with the level of responsibility we both have, what with me running the show here and Sophia opening her third store this week. It's pretty great."

"Glad to hear it. What's your background?" Ben asked.

"Well, I was a manager at a franchise flower shop during college. I did the ordering of materials, took orders from customers, and scheduled the people and the deliveries. It gave me a ton of experience in management and I credit it with landing me this job."

"I see," Ben said. "So, your experience is mostly in a company that had a really well-defined system?"

"Oh, yes, they had published processes, procedure manuals and even a cool app that gave me a management checklist of tasks that needed to be done each day." Tia replied.

Ben asked inquisitively, "And does that differ from working here?"

Tia laughed nervously and lowered her voice, "Yeah, here we don't really have that. We focus more on sales and getting orders out. We don't really have a system we follow. We rely upon our people to 'know how to get things done.' We like to say that, to work here, you have to have a good memory because things move fast and you have a lot of things coming at you."

"That sounds like the average business, then. Tia, can I ask you a few questions and be honest with you?"

"Sure, Ben."

"The approach you all are using here is flawed and those flaws are causing a lot of financial headaches. Profits are down, and Susan and Steve are concerned. They brought me into help."

"Profits are down? Ben, how is that possible?" Tia asked with a confused look on her face. "We are busier than ever! We run more shifts, more hours, more people and, on the whole, the people working here are really solid. At least, those they hired in the last year are so much better than the people we used to hire. How could we possibly be worse off, Ben?"

"Tia, I understand your frustration. You and your team are working harder than ever, but the reality is the team is less proficient and efficient now than they were in the past. Some of that likely has to do with them going faster and spending less attention to the details. Some of it could be the workers have gotten sloppy and some of it is that management isn't really paying attention."

"Ben, that may be true. And, if it wasn't for Sophia always singing your praises, I might be less inclined to hear you out. But your reputation proceeds you and I want to learn!"

"Excellent, Tia. First, let me see what you work on each day."

The two walked back to Tia's cubicle, where she pulled up another chair so she and Ben could both sit facing her computer screens.

"OK, Ben. Each day when I arrive, I have this report on my desk that shows me all the orders that need to ship today. I then take each of those line items and enter them into this spreadsheet to create a schedule for the lines. Each order has a corresponding job jacket that is in the filing cabinet across the hallway in the sales department."

Ben listened intently while Tia continued. "The salespeople take the orders, fill out the order forms and hand them to Accounting. Accounting takes those orders and enters them in the system. The sales person also puts pertinent data, like colors or special requests, in a job jacket they file in their main office. I get a report each morning from accounting that allows me to create the schedule and retrieve the job jackets. I put everything together, schedule it all, and then I stack them by production lines."

Tia took a breath and continued. "Each line leader stops here when they arrive and pull the job jackets for their line. Then, when their team arrives, they all go and pull the parts and pieces they will need for the first job jacket and get started.

"As the work is completed for the first job jacket, the line lead goes and retrieves the materials for the next order and keeps feeding the line. Does that make sense, Ben?"

"Well, it makes products. Not sure it makes sense." Ben emphasized the word sense in a way that Tia was unsure if he meant cents like dollars and cents or sense like logic. Either way, she realized both fit the situation.

Ben continued. "Can you pull up that Excel spreadsheet you use?"

"Sure, Ben, here it is."

Ben asked, "How long does this morning ritual of yours take, entering the orders into the sheet pulling the jackets, separating them by line, and then handing them out as lead's arrive?"

"For the most part, it takes me about an hour. I get here at 6 a.m., and the leads show up at 6:45 to get their job jackets."

"And how long does the Excel spreadsheet take?" Ben asked.

"Not long, maybe 20 minutes." Tia responded.

Ben shook his head with acknowledgement and asked, "And why, may I ask, do you get a paper printout of the orders that need to be produced that day? Why not an Excel spreadsheet of those jobs so you can just work out of that sheet?"

"Oh, that's simple, Ben," Tia replied. "I don't have access to the accounting system. So, the accounting department just prints me off the order sheet and I enter them here."

Ben looked confused. "Why in the world do you not have access to that system, or why is accounting printing this versus emailing?"

"Well, Ben, from what I understand there are some profit numbers on that report. The accounting department hides those columns then prints the report for me."

"I see," said Ben. "Let me look into that for you. Do you know if sales have access to enter their orders into the accounting system or ..."

Tia interrupted, "Oh, no, they don't see that information, either. It's top secret. They do manual orders for each sale and then send them to accounting for input."

"Aha, OK, let me chat with accounting on that." Ben made a note in his iPad.

"Tia," Ben continued, "what of the 8 areas of waste we talked about on the floor would you say this manual process falls into?"

Tia looked at her notebook. "Ben, from my perspective, this feels like over-processing. There are so many extra steps here and, although they each only take a few moments, they add up."

"Sounds right to me. Too many steps and each step takes time. What's the old saying? Time is money!"

Ben continued, "Tia, tell me more about your day-to-day activities."

"Overall, Ben, that process fills my 6-7 a.m. Once that is all resolved for the day, I usually grab my clipboard and head out to the floor to get a feel for inventory levels."

"OK, Tia, lets head out and look at those."

Ben followed Tia out to the floor, past the production lines and into a sea of floor-to-ceiling pallet racks stacked full of inventory items.

"Back here is where we maintain the inventory," Tia said as she turned to Ben. "When I come back here, I am looking at levels of inventory that need attended to. See, for instance, this paper stock is looking low—I need to order some of that."

Ben piped in. "So how many days' inventory is on hand right now?"

"Sorry, Ben, I am not following you," Tia said, looking for more information.

Ben replied, "If you could not get access to materials temporarily—how long could you still produce products?"

A light went off with Tia. "Ben, that really depends on the product. Some items we would probably run out of in a month, others might take a year."

"A year!?" Ben said in a loud voice, almost yelling. Alarmed, Tia, took a step back. "Tia," Ben continued, "how in the world do we have one-year worth of inventory on hand for a product we make?"

Tia continued cautiously. "Well, there are only a few items like that and the reason we have so many is that we got a killer deal on them, like these fasteners here. If we bought six or more pallets, we got a 10% discount, so we jumped on that deal. Steve said those savings would help our Cost of Goods. But most of these other items turn pretty quickly."

"Tia, what do you mean by 'pretty quickly'? For instance, this paper stock—when it the last time you ordered it and do you use it a lot?

"Ben, we do use it, frequently. At least once a week, we run the big printer in the back and produce all our product tags for the week."

"And when is the last time you ordered this paper stock?" Ben asked.

"That I don't know, Ben. Let me ask Sara in accounting."

Tia grabbed the walkie-talkie from her belt and paged Sara.

"Hey Sara, can you tell me the last time we ordered paper stock and how much of it we got?"

"Sure thing, Tia, give me a second." There was a pause as the clicking of Sara's computer keyboard came faintly over the speaker mic. "Looks like last order was January 4th of this year. Six pallets. That all you need?"

"Yes, thanks, Sara." Tia snapped off the volume on her walkie-talkie. "You hear that, Ben?"

"I sure did," Ben replied. "So how many pallets do we have left here? I count three."

Tia nodded her head.

"So, Tia, let's do the math. You ordered six pallets, six months back and you have three pallets left."

"Yeah, that is a problem, huh Ben? Right now, according to how much we have used, I have six months-worth on hand, PLUS I have all the tags we ran just yesterday that will last me all week. 27 weeks of inventory are on hand!"

"Precisely. Might that be a little excessive?" Ben said with a hint of sarcasm. "But let's talk this through, Tia. How long does it take to get this paper stock, from the time you order it until the time it delivers?"

"I can get paper stock first thing next morning, as long as I order before 3 p.m.," Tia replied.

Ben then asked, "And what is the minimum quantity they will allow you to purchase?"

"I can get as little as two boxes at a time, although," Tia emphasized the next point, "the vendor charges us more for the smaller orders."

"OK, Tia, a couple things we can do here. First, we need not bother with ordering paper stock until the end of the year. Keep your eye on it and, if the level falls below one week, then you need to take action. As long as there is enough for 24 hours, the inventory level is not critical since you can get material more quickly than that."

Tia shook her head understanding that Ben was correct.

"On the price of the material we need to look at what percent savings there is between buying a smaller quantity or a larger one. For the most part, the discount won't be enough to make buying the larger quantity worthwhile.

"Think about it this way. We used cash on hand in January to buy this paper that now is just sitting here and will be for the next six months. Most businesses do not have the luxury on lots of cash on hand. They manage the flow of cash in and out of the business on a daily basis and, if that cash is running low, they go to their bank and borrow money to make up the shortfalls.

"I don't know for sure, but I can almost guarantee Susan and Steve do that same process. So that means, to save a few percent, we had to borrow money at a higher rate from the bank to do that. That rarely makes sense.

"The other thing is this. You will still use six pallets this year, right?"

"Correct." Tia responded.

Ben continued, "So why not talk to the vendor end of the year and tell them you still will buy all six pallets next year, but you just want them to ship them only as you need them.

"I'm willing to bet the sales guy on that side will give you the same discount, since you are still buying the same amount. You are just paying for it and having it delivered over time versus all at once. You might pay a bit more for delivery, but you might not. In most cases, this makes sense."

"Ben!" Tia said enthusiastically. "That does make sense. It helps the company and allows me more space here in the warehouse. That's space we can use for other processes, machines, and staging for shipping."

"Glad you see it, Tia. So, let me ask you, do you think this paper stock is an anomaly or do you believe other back stocked materials are similar?"

Tia chuckled. "I bet nearly all of the materials are like this. Some might be closer to a month or two, but since those materials are found locally, I don't need to order them in quantity. I just need them when we need them."

"Exactly, Tia, the term for that process is Just in Time inventory. Why buy, store, and move around materials you don't need right now? In Japan, many companies buy only enough material for that workday or work shift and are in a constant state of replenishment. That might be a bit much for the factory here, but it's a goal to work towards.

"There's another real advantage, too. Currently, you're buying materials based on the orders you make today. But what happens if a design is discontinued or eliminated?"

"Ben, we know all about that! Let me show you something." Tia motioned to Ben to follow her.

Tia walked Ben back deeper into the warehouse. They turned a corner to face a massive wall of premade product, pallet racks 30 feet high and 50 feet long stacked completely full of boxed products.

"What in the world is this, Tia?" Ben exclaimed.

Tia sat on the edge of a big box and continued. "The story goes that, two years back, we had a new product idea. We assumed it would be a hot seller for Black Friday, so we made a bunch of inventories in anticipation of the holiday rush. Unfortunately, the demand wasn't there and we got stuck with all these products. We eventually pushed them here in the back and put them for sale on

Amazon. They do sell on Amazon—usually about 5-10 a month. Problem is, there are over 2,500 of them still left. The joke is we have to leave a note on the pallets to remind the people that work here after we all retire to keep selling them."

"Wow," Ben replied wide-eyed. "Not sure if I have ever seen anything like this, Tia. Let me talk with Steve about it."

Ben's eyes surveyed the length of the warehouse. "Can we dig just a little deeper here? Can you show me the other items you inventory?"

"Sure, let's go take a look at the hardware cage and paint area."

As they walked, Ben jotted a few more notes on his iPad.

Chapter 5

Motion & Skills

"OK, Ben," Tia said, as they arrived at a large metal fenced-in area with a large sliding gate on it. "This is the hardware coral and paint storage. We keep these items in this locked area because they are high value.

"Over here we have hardware, nuts, bolts, fasteners, plugs—all the items the lines might need to complete a project.

"And on this side, we have paint. The painting department uses these cans on items we produce that need a coat of paint."

Ben immediately headed to the paint cans. He picked them up, shook them, and asked Tia "How long is paint good for? A few years?"

"I believe so, Ben. An 'opened' date should be written on the top cover there. And, if I'm not mistaken, the paint quality is affected after three years, if the can was sealed correctly."

"What about this can here, Tia? It was opened December 11th, 2010. And this one; it's only two years old, but shake it."

Tia shook the can, and there was no noise. The lid was put on incorrectly and the paint had dried out.

"I dunno, Ben, I just count them. I never really looked at them," Tia replied.

"These expired and useless materials are still in inventory?" Ben asked.

Tia replied, "Yes, they are. And I don't really feel comfortable throwing them out. We paid for those materials and I'd be afraid Steve would be upset if he saw me doing that."

"I understand that," Ben said with a nod. "Problem is there is no procedure here. Getting rid of things can be tough if you are a manager. At some point in time we paid for that and what authority do you have to throw it out!"

"Exactly, Ben. I just want to do a good job. I don't want any trouble, and throwing away inventory is not in my job description. No one ever gave me permission to do that."

Ben continued, "Tia, do you think you have the skills to determine what is good, usable inventory and what is not?"

"Of course, Ben who couldn't?" Tia's expression darkened with a frown. "If an item is out of date or no longer functional, I think even a small child could sort out what is good or bad."

"Tia, I didn't mean to offend you; my point was another one of the Enemies. You currently have the skills—heck everyone here does—but for some reason the company either has a hidden expectation that you can't use those skills, or there is a misunderstanding on what we have in inventory and the materials' lifespan."

"Tia, I will work on that with the Executive team. They need to be willing to create a policy that allows you and your teams to use your expertise and skills without fear of repercussions."

Ben changed the subject. "Now, as far as these fasteners go—you saw what we did back in the pallet racks; we need to do the same here. How many do we use each day? How long does it take to get them? Then, from that information, we can determine what the reorder point is. If it hasn't reached that point, we do not order it.

"There's one other thing I noticed while we were over here with the paint. Twice, I saw line leads rush in here, grab a handful or box full of something, and rush back out. What is that all about?"

Tia replied, "When the line leads need materials, they go and pull them to keep the line flowing. Hardware is part of that. They come over here and get what they need."

"And what do they need?" Ben asked.

"Materials, Ben?" Tia asked in a questioning tone, and then continued to answer her own question. "They need them for the line."

"Yes," Ben acknowledged the answer, driving Tia to dig in further. "But how do they know how many? And do they keep any on hand?"

Tia replied, "Basically, no. They pull hardware based on what they think they will need for the order."

"Think, or know?" Ben questioned.

"Ben, I don't know. I believe they estimate what they think they will need based on their experience."

"One other question, Tia," Ben asked. "Why is this hardware and paint in a cage?"

"To protect our valuable resources, I guess," replied Tia.

"Then why isn't it locked? We walked right in. The line leads walked right in, too, and took what they need. What is the purpose of a cage with a lock when you leave the cage unlocked?"

Tia replied, "Well, we do lock it at night. I open it up each morning when I get it. We used to have it locked all the time and the line leads had keys, but because they were always in a hurry to get materials and sometimes forgot or lost their keys, it just made more sense to keep it unlocked during business hours."

Ben asked with a chuckle, "So we lock it at night when no one is here to protect the assets, yet when employees, customers, delivery people, and vendors are here the cage is wide open?"

"I guess that makes no sense, huh?" Tia shrugged.

"Tia, it doesn't make any sense at all. But the bigger problem is how your leads are rushing in and out of here for every job.

"Look at the location of the lines. Line 1 is close—what, maybe 40 feet from the cage? Line 5 is probably 100 feet away. How many times a day does Line 5 lead come over here? 10-12?"

"Some days, more than that. Some days it could be 20 times," replied Tia.

Ben continued. "So, we have our most experienced person rushing over here 20 times a day to get materials that are in a cage because they are high value, but the cage is unlocked?"

"Ugh," Tia grunted, "this is insane! Add that to the number of trips to get other materials, and poor Julio on Line 5 is getting a serious workout!"

"Ever think that might be why Julio is as fit as he is?" Ben laughed, while looking over at Line 5 and seeing how Julio resembled a lean boxer on weigh-in day. "He literally doesn't need to go to the gym; his workout is rushing around this place. Worse, I bet Julio and the other leads are in their roles because they are good, likely the best on the line."

Tia nodded. "Absolutely, they are the backbone. They know every product, every workstation, and help us clear bottlenecks"

Ben inquired, "How can they do that while running their daily marathon?"

Tia shook her head, acknowledging how silly it all seemed.

"Tia," Ben continued, "what Enemy is this?"

"I don't know, Ben. Is it Transportation, since people are rushing around trying to get inventory and carry it back to their line? Or is it Motion?"

Ben replied with a smile, "Good point, Tia. As a rule, we want to think of transportation in two ways; internal and external. Events such as the steps in getting materials, parts, and pieces to the workspace where value is added are internal. This also can include moving the parts, pieces, code, or data to advance the project to or from a step in the process in order for more work to be done. External transportation is the movement of materials or data to the facility, or the logistics of moving the final product to the customer or distributor.

"Motion, on the other hand, is the moving and turning of people or materials once they are in the workspace; bending, lifting, downloading, unzipping, etc.

"The challenge with internal transportation is that it can be the costliest of Enemies, so it is something you must always be conscious of. When you see a person or material moving, you have to ask yourself Why."

Ben continued, "Tia, let me tell you about the work/waste paradox. It goes like this:

"Only a fraction of the work done at work, is work!"

Tia shook her head as if it was the first time she'd ever thought about something happening at work not qualifying as work.

Ben waited a few moments then continued. "For the most part, people believe that work is from the time you clock in until the time you leave. But that isn't true. Work is the time you spend adding value to customers.

"You and your leads are busy—incredibly busy—but much of your activity is not adding value to the customer. No customer would pay for your leads to rush back and forth all day. No, they pay for the product, the quality of design, the materials, and the craftsmanship. When Julio or any of the others perform tasks like those we just saw, they are not working; they are not providing value.

"As the leader, you need to understand the difference between work and waste, and strive to create systems that bring order to the chaos. Strive to find ways that keep your people working, not doing unimportant tasks.

"Now, getting materials is important, but there are better ways to do it. A picker might be one way; a full-time person that has a walkie-talkie and is getting the materials from inventory to the line."

Tia glanced up and to the right over Ben shoulder as she imagined her life and the factory with less chaos and more order.

Ben continued. "A change in shifts is another approach. An early shift starts a bit earlier and stocks up materials on the line for the entire shift or for a half a shift, then replenishes those materials at intervals. Or, maybe you work with the leads to estimate the need for the day and they come in a few minutes early and collect those things. Heck, maybe the big cage needs to become smaller cages located within hand's reach of the line leads."

Tia replied, "Ben, that makes so much sense, but our lines are too tight. Look at the walkways and pathways where pallets and carts can get through—there is no place to put inventory on the floor."

Ben replied in a reassuring tone, "Tia, I agree under this current layout there is no way to place materials next to the lines. But, imagine for a moment we were just moving in and setting this place up from scratch. What would do you do differently in the layout, keeping in mind the need to feed the lines?"

"Well, first thing I would do is shift the lines down 20 feet from the current walkway. That would allow more room for materials at the front of the line. I would probably also make more space between the lines so workers could have hardware and materials at hand's reach."

"Great ideas, Tia. So, what is stopping you from making that change?" Ben asked.

"Lots of things. First, Susan and Steve are reluctant right now to spend money. Second, the machines are easy to move—they are on rollers—but look at the power drops. Some of these machines need high voltage power and the outlets are right beside the machines. It just isn't possible."

Ben replied, "I get that, but let's not approach these changes as costs but as savings. Let's map out how much time is spent running around and then determine how much time and money is wasted doing those things.

"Next, we have to remember that power is moveable. Let's say we determine the relocation of the lines is feasible and financially viable in the long term. We then need to take the costs of moving the equipment into consideration and find out how long it would take the move to pay for itself in savings. You might be surprised."

Ben continued, "I recently worked on a facility that found it would cost $500 to move a machine, relocate the power, and have a technician re-level it. Our analysis showed a $2,500 per week savings by making the move. That was a no-brainer."

Tia shook her head and appeared as if she was daydreaming about how this might all work.

Ben gave Tia a moment, then continued. "Sometimes the payback can be weeks or months, but for the most part, it is almost always worth moving something to improve efficiency and cut waste. Automating things can be expensive, but moving a machine or a line is an easy way to improve productivity and reduce waste of motion."

Tia shook her head. "Wow, that is great. I had never even considered doing that. So, should I do some sort of analysis that shows the value to Susan and Steve?"

"Yes, but to do it you need to do a spaghetti diagram that shows where people move and why. Measure out the number of feet they walk or move things and consider all the advantages in production time—less walking, less damage to materials, fewer materials disappearing, etc.

"If you aren't familiar with it, a spaghetti diagram is just a floor plan of the facility and lines drawn on it showing the paths people move. Just Google spaghetti diagram, Tia, and you will get a whole bunch of examples.

"You can use a rolling measure wheel to determine how many feet people and items are moving. Once you have done that, you can draw out the new floor plan and imagine how people would move through that layout. In the end, you just count the feet on both models and you can see the improvement.

"Before you finalize that plan, you show it to the people who it will affect. In this instance, it's the line leads. Show them the plan, have them ask questions, let them move things, and see if it improves flow. Get as much feedback as possible and make sure everyone has a voice. That might mean asking for both verbal and written ideas; some people aren't comfortable sharing in a group. So, make sure you do everything you can to capture everything you can.

"This is great, Ben. Can I give you a little recap of what I need to be working on? I made a few notes on my iPad."

"Sure, fire away, Tia."

Tia continued, "First, I need to understand how much material we have on hand and how often it depletes.

"Second, I need to find out how long it takes us to get material in days.

"Then I run the math to determine how many days' worth of inventory to keep on hand and what my reorder point is."

Ben nodded in agreement.

"Once I have that data, I can wait on a material reaching the reorder point, then negotiate with the vendor on our projected volume for the year. But I want to set up a payment and delivery schedule that aligns with the demand for the material—try to make materials as Just in Time as possible. Correct?" asked Tia.

"Correct," Ben answered.

Tia continued, "Next, I need to do a spaghetti diagram to determine where people are going and the movement of materials and people.

"From that I can begin thinking about a better layout—one that would eliminate as much waste as possible and get my people focused on work, not walking.

"Once I have a new layout, I imagine how the material and people would flow through it and I recount the number of feet they move. From that I can share the diagram with my people, capture their ideas and, finally, determine the improvements I want to present to Susan and Steve."

Tia concluded, "Always remember the work/waste paradox—only a fraction of the work done at work, is work."

"You got it, Tia," Ben replied. "Another thing to consider on the spaghetti diagram is rethinking your inventory. You are about to have far less of it on hand. So, make sure you consider that in your new layout. Moving the inventory racks 20, 30 or even 40 feet might be a viable solution and a better use of the space."

Tia shook her head and made a note of the idea.

"And my takeaways are," Ben replied and listed them off:

Speak with accounting about report access and data entry for sales.

Run the math on the cost to the company for both Tia and sales people not having access.

How much inventory is on hand?

What is the rent per square foot on the building?

"Any questions, Tia?" Ben asked.

"Just two. First, how do I find the time to do these things? And second—there is a lot of math here, huh?"

Ben replied, "Yes, there is a lot of math, but it's basic addition and subtraction, multiplication and division. You use Excel every day, Tia. You should be fine."

"Oh, I don't doubt it! I was an ace at math in school, but my parents always told me I would never use it once I graduated. I'm just happy they were wrong!"

"As for the question of time," Ben added, "you are right, this will take some time. But, trust me, it will take far less time than continuing on the existing path. Think about the hours of frustration, management, of fires, of line slowdowns that your investment will reduce. Ten to fifteen hours of time analyzing this will pay off in spades, not just for the company, but also for you personally and professionally.

"I also have a tool I can teach you that will help. It's called the Block, Tackle, or Handoff."

"Sounds like football," Tia replied.

"It certainly does", Ben chuckled. "Here is how it works: each day you set apart at least one 25-minute block of time where you can work uninterrupted. During that time, you do focused work, like creating these diagrams and building these spreadsheets. During that time, you can only focus on those tasks; no emails, no looking at your phone, no interruptions at all, period.

"Tell your people that you are not available at that time and the only excuse to interrupt you is 'blood or fire.' There is nothing more important than that uninterrupted time. I always suggest that leaders have a minimum of two of those blocked time-periods each day.

"Then when things arise throughout the day, you must ask yourself three questions:

1. Can I handle this in my blocks?
2. Must I tackle this right now?
3. Can I hand this task off and delegate someone to handle it?

"Tia, what you will quickly find is that you will accomplish a tremendous amount during your blocks, as you are completely focused on the tasks at hand. You will also better manage your time by asking the questions and determining what needs your immediate attention, what can wait, and what you can pass off to someone else.

"The Block, Tackle, or Handoff is a simple tool but one of the most powerful in your management tool belt."

Tia smiled and said, "I love this. It's so simple, but I can see how it gives me more time to handle the things I need to do to help turn this place around. Thanks, Ben!"

Ben shook Tia's hand and headed up to the front offices.

The Playbook

Ben has introduced a number of tools and concepts by this point. Let's review them.

The Fishbowl A leaky fishbowl cannot be resolved by adding water or replacing fish. It can only be resolved by repairing the leaks in the bowl. Modern management approaches the fishbowl problem by insisting that more revenue and upgraded or better-trained employees are the solution, even when logic tells us that only rational solution is to focus on fixing the bowl.

The Huddle is covered in other Playbook works. It is a brief standup meeting that is done at least once each day. The objective is to talk about successes, set goals for the day, and uncover barriers in the process.

The employees should do 95% or more of the talking. The manager is just there to facilitate and find problems they need to address.

The Walkabout Every manager, without exception, should walk the floor where the work is being done AT LEAST twice each day. The point of the walk is to be present, to show the team you are paying attention, and to inspect the work being done. The Walkabout is NEVER confrontational; it is for information gathering, using the senses of the manager to walk around, develop relationships and ask questions.

People will only respect what you inspect.

The Enemies of EBITDA These are the eight areas in every business where waste is found. Transportation, Inventory, Motion, Waiting, Over-production, Over-processing, Defects, and Skills. These are the focus of this book, but there are three other areas that the author also considers enemies.

First, the enemy of Asymmetry; a business that does not have a consist flow of business or materials both in and out of the business. Seasonality, end-of-the-month order rushes, etc. all make a business asymmetrical, and asymmetrical businesses tend to struggle with wages and cost overruns.

Second, the enemy of Deviation; deviation is when the people in a company are not following a process and creating extra steps. Even if well-meaning, unchecked deviation can wreak havoc on a company. An extra, undocumented step creates an environment where scale is impossible because the people doing the jobs are the only ones that know the steps of the process. Furthermore, those extra steps or deviations may not be beneficial in light of the entire process. Any change to process requires insight and thought about the outcomes that change effects.

Last, the enemy of Excess Capacity. Do elements of your business only generate revenue when you are there actively working in or on them? Or do meeting rooms, machines, etc., sit empty at any time throughout the day and night? If so, then consider the creative ways you can use those spaces and equipment to increase your business.

An empty meeting room could be rented for $25-$50 per hour to entrepreneurs or out of town business persons.

A machine sitting dormant at night might be rented out or operated by your team on behalf of another company.

We have seen CNC machines go from running 8 hours a day for the company to 24 hours a day by the company on behalf of another that cannot afford a CNC, has a machine down, or has a large order.

A café that closes after lunch might find a chef wanting to start a dinner restaurant. By swapping out the sign at night, and changing the linen and lighting, those restaurants might find that sharing the costs of the facility and staff makes them both more profitable.

The 5 Why's Most managers see a problem and try to solve it. The purpose of the 5 Why's is to stop that from happening and focus instead on why the problem started in the first place, asking "Why?" over and over about the problem until you expose its root cause. By solving the root cause, you resolve the problem permanently.

Just in Time Inventory Holding onto old inventory or raw materials is almost always a bad idea. Having on hand what you need for that week, day or, ideally, shift is the optimal way to save space and money. Inventory of any sort costs money, be it real raw materials or items you just never got around to purging or liquidating, or as with businesses that write code, deleting or archiving.

As with a computer, the more stuff you keep on it the slower the machine runs. The same is true of every business. Don't fall into the idea of sunk costs. If a material, product, or file no longer brings value, get rid of it.

Process Mapping/Spaghetti Diagrams Motion and transportation can kill a company. Motion is the little things we do in our workspace while adding value, things such as bending, turning, or running to the printer. These things add up, and many occurrences result in repetitive stress and overuse injuries. They contribute to waste because, when people aren't feeling there best—when they are tired, sore, or injured—their rate of work slows down, or they avoid doing critical tasks because of their pain. Optimizing workspaces produces better outcomes.

Transportation can be both internal and external. You must combat both. External logistics can often be resolved by having a tighter review process on costs, better negotiations, or thinking about why you do things the way you do. Combining shipment, having pickup windows, only shipping on certain days of the week, etc., can all help reduce costs and improve margins.

Internal Transportation, i.e., the steps people take to complete the work, is from our perspective the area where manufacturing companies need the most help. The feeding of lines, the movement of materials, and the access to inventory can and usually does translate into thousands of hours of wasted steps.

Diagramming, mapping, and process analysis are great tools to combat these enemies.

The Block, Tackle, or Handoff

Any time you face a new task, you must ask yourself three questions:

1. Can I handle this in my blocks?
2. Must I tackle this right now?
3. Can I hand this task off and delegate someone to handle it?

Setting apart time to get things done is the best way to control time.

Chapter 6

"Steve, got a second?" Ben asked as he stuck his head in Steve's door.

"Sure Ben, what's up?"

"Steve, I really enjoyed my time with Tia. She's really smart and very loyal. Really wants to make an impact."

"Ben, I'm truly glad to hear that. Did you learn anything more during your time with her?"

Ben headed over to the chair in front of Steve's desk, sat down, and pulled out his iPad.

"Lots, Steve. Can you take a few notes? Tia and I will need some things from you.

"First, what is the cost per square footage on this building; rent or mortgage, utilities, etc.?

Steve replied, "Rent is at fifty cents per square foot for the whole facility. Utilities over the course of the year are fourteen cents per square foot, understanding that in the winter it is about half that, but in the summer with the Phoenix heat it can be as high as double that."

Ben jotted that down and continued his questioning. "Next, I want to ask you a question about inventory. If an inventory item is expired or no longer usable—say old paint or materials that have expired or no longer are part of the process—does Tia have permission to discard them?"

"Hmm, can you give me a specific example, Ben?"

"Sure. We have paint in the materials cage that is completely dried out and unusable. Is that a material that can be discarded?"

Steve looked surprised. "Of course that can be thrown out. Why would keep that?"

Ben continued, "How about outdated paint? Say the manufacturer tells us that the material is only good for three years after opening. At what point can it be recycled?"

"Well, do we believe the manufacturer? I guess they should know, but the question is does it just start to degrade at that point or do we have six months after that expiration to use it?"

"Good question, Steve, and I do not know the answer, but if there is a chance that paint used after the expiration date is a lower quality, should we use it? Or does using it run a risk that the client will be unsatisfied if the color is not precise?"

"Ahh," Steve grunted, "I see the point. To save a few dollars in saving things we risk opening ourselves up to re-doing a job to make it right for the customer. So then, the answer is, if the material has an expiration date, at the expiration date it needs to come out of inventory and be reported to accounting."

"Exactly," Ben said. "So, starting today, Tia has the authority to remove items that are no longer usable or have expired?"

Though Ben formed it as a question, Steve knew it wasn't really a question. "Yes, absolutely," he replied. "She just needs to provide accounting with a report of what is being removed."

Ben continued. "Next, remember from our conversation on the floor that you need to determine an acceptable rate of over runs? Gianni said 3-5% was standard, but as you saw it as far above that. Furthermore, is 3-5% even needed?"

Steve replied, "Got it, Ben, I have some of my team pulling numbers on what or if there has ever been any communication to the floor on overruns. We are also casually polling the operators to see what they believe is the right number. Once that is done, we will create a worksheet of what people perceive. Then we will dig into the garbage and get to the bottom of this."

Excellent," Ben replied. "Just keep in mind that this is not about judgement. This is not the operator's fault. This is on management. Don't go stomping around acting like this is on them. This is on you."

Steve squirmed a bit in his seat knowing Ben was right and feeling the invisible, yet palpable weight of accountability resting on his shoulders.

Ben continued. "Not saying this to make you feel uncomfortable. But I am glad it has."

Steve squirmed a bit more in his seat.

"You just need to approach this humbly. Recognize that you are the leader and, as the leader, the buck stops with you, Senior Management."

Ben relaxed his expression and leaned back in his chair. "Enough of that, you know what you need to do. Find out the right number, set a new standard, talk to the vendor, talk to the operators, try it yourself and then make it a standard. But always remember, a standard is the standard for today. Incremental improvement is always the goal. Once this is done, empower your people to find ways to improve that process. Every. Single. Day."

Steve acknowledged what Ben was saying through both his expression and his demeanor.

Ben continued his dialogue. "This is not an infomercial; we do not set it and forget it. We improve it in perpetuity."

Steve sat back in his chair for a moment and pondered an existence of continuous improvement, where profit margins and proficiency increased every day as if by design.

As Steve sat forward again, he looked at Ben and asked, "Ben, how do we sustain that? Constant change can be exhausting and expensive. And won't we eventually perfect things?"

"Unlikely," Ben replied to the second half of Steve's question. "There is no perfect state. There is always room to improve." Ben allowed that to linger in the air for a second so Steve could soak it in and likely disagree, then Ben continued. "We sustain by making improvement part of the system. We challenge ourselves and our people to always look for small improvements. This process we are embarking on will find many ways to improve the business by 10% or 20% in a specific area, but those will cost money and will cause some level of disruption. Disruption is OK occasionally, but for the most part, you want to maintain some symmetry to the business and the process. Therefore, once we complete this project, the day-to-day improvement goal is simply 1%. 1% better every day. That needs to become your rally cry for your people and for yourself. A challenge that drives you. How can we make this 1% better today, tomorrow, and every day thereafter?

"This 1% goal will convert your laborers into knowledge workers. Instead of mindlessly performing a task because it is 'part of their job', they will begin looking for incremental improvements. Not disruptions mind you. There is a time and place for that, of course, but for the most part small incremental improvements do not disrupt the symmetry of the business. They aren't adeviation to the process; they are, in fact, leaning the whole process out."

Steve thought for a moment about how there was a difference between disruptive innovation and retooling of the business, and the incremental improvement of every day. Being an accounting guy, Steve looked back to Ben.

"Ben, do I have my math right here. 1% improvement every day is, what, 3,600% or more annualized?"

"Close, Steve!" Ben said excitedly. "More like 3,800%!"

"I see it now Ben, but the reality is, how long can you sustain that level of improvement? Everything eventually reaches perfection, no?"

Steve leaned in hoping either for a sage response, or maybe deep inside he was hoping to have stumped the master.

Ben laughed a bit. "Steve, can I tell you a little secret? One that I rarely share. One that most people never ask about because, once they understand the math, they are so overwhelmed they never even consider the possibility of reaching perfection."

"Share away," Steve said as he waited for some sage advice.

"Ohno." Ben whispered.

"Oh what?" Steve said with a bit of disappointment to his voice.

"Taiichi Ohno." Ben said, as if Steve would understand.

Steve thought for a moment and realized that Ohno was the founder of the famed Toyota Production System. "Yes, of course, Taiichi Ohno was the creator of much of what we call continuous improvement. But what does that have to do with reaching perfection?"

Ben began to narrate in voice that sounded like the preface of a fairytale. "Ohno had a system of small incremental improvement and empowering his people to collect the data; to be the eyes of his system, to report to him like spies, always looking, always searching for deviation, asymmetry, and waste. Ohno's people were knowledge workers who just happened to work with their hands in assembling cars. And those people were diligent in their pursuit of gathering information. So diligent, perhaps, that at times Ohno would find they'd run out of ideas—they could find no more ways to improve."

Steve leaned in even further waiting for the conclusion of the story and the explanation of how this all tied together.

"Then Ohno would remove resources from the process in order to start the process of improvement all over again."

Steve nearly gasped. "I get it!" He would perfect the system, and then remove resources from the system to perfect it again! Brilliant."

Ben continued, proud that Steve understood. "Ohno would do this over and over again. Removing resources, people, shortening timelines, and time and time again his team would perfect the process, each time with less and less resources.

"Ohno's name is fitting and I use it as the name of the tool that described the feeling we get when we use it. Oh No! He's taking resources again."

Steve let out some uproarious laughter and smacked his desk. "Brilliant, Ben, brilliant! But seriously, Ben how long can the cycle continue? Is it ever perfected?"

"Of course, Steve. At some point you will reach," Ben held up his fingers in air quotes and spoke the word, "nirvana."

Ben continued. "From my experience you can almost always do 3-5 cycles of Ohno's after a process is perfected. Let's say we remove 10% of the resources each round. That would mean, AFTER we are satisfied that part of the system is optimal and perfected, we are still able to reduce and perfect it 30-50% more!"

"My God, Ben, is that truly even possible here?" Steve asked searching for the answer.

Ben replied, "Maybe, maybe not. But let's assume for a moment that you are different than my other clients and I am 90% wrong about the level of improvement you could make over time. Would you still do it?"

Steve thought for a split second and laughed. "Of course, Ben, you can miss the mark by a mile and still hit the target with those numbers."

Ben continued. "Glad that makes sense, Steve. Mind if I get back my list?"

"Sure, sure go ahead."

"Steve, first we need a sit down with your department."

Steve nodded.

Ben added, "There seems to be a control issue with the department and likely it isn't one that is intentionally disruptive. But it is causing some problems.

"For instance, did you know that neither sales nor Tia have access to the accounting system to either enter in orders or to generate the reports they need to schedule and fulfill orders?"

Steve replied, "I knew that we generated reports and did data entry but I wasn't aware that it was a big deal or a bottleneck."

"Well, it is," Ben replied. "Tia has to wait upon reports, then take that data and reenter all of it into the schedule, then pull the job jackets from sales, combine them all together, schedule the production lines, and hand out the assignments. All because accounting is afraid; afraid she will see the margin numbers."

Steve jumped in. "That doesn't make a lick of sense. Our permissions on that system are hierarchical. We can limit what anyone sees or enters. Are you telling me that Tia does this process manually and repeats all the data entry because she doesn't have the proper report access?"

"Exactly, Steve and, worse, the salespeople are filling out paper order forms and handing them off to accounting so they can enter the data. Then the sale team keeps their job jackets so Tia can retrieve them.

"Steve, count it up. Sales people enters data into order form, Accounting enters identical data into the system, Tia enters identical data into her schedules. Then Tia has to retrieve the parts and pieces that are not included in the order forms but found in a job jacket the sales team created. Does that make any sense to you?"

"None," Steve said angrily. "Why in the world isn't it seamless? Sales enters data that passes to Tia and Accounting, and if there are elements of the job that sales are not entering, we just need to create a field in the system to allow them to enter it there. I can see this not only being a bottleneck, but it brings up a much bigger question."

Ben inquired, "And that is?"

Steve explained, "Special requests are usually things we are doing as a premium service. Special handling, extra features, expedited shipping, that sort of thing. If that data is not passed to Accounting, is it being billed? Likely not!" Steve shook his head as if he were disgusted. "Think about it, Ben. We are not making profit and we are possibly giving away our premium services, for," Steve slowed his tone of speech and spelled it out, "F–R–E–E."

Ben allowed the air to settle in the room and spoke. "Steve, it's easy to get upset about the past. But the past will not solve this. We need to act, now, today and resolve this problem going forward. Can you make a call to accounting and see if they can set up the hierarchy?"

"Yes," Steve replied, "right after our meeting. Then I will head down to talk with Tia and the sales team about the changes."

"Excellent," Ben replied. "Just for purpose of understanding the impact of this change, let me ask you a few questions.

"First, Tia tells me it takes her 20 minutes to copy the report and probably 10 to round up the job jackets. How long do you think it takes sales to fill out the order form and accounting to enter it?"

Steve replied, "I'd say 5 minutes for each. 5 for sales, 5 for accounting."

"And how many orders each day?" Ben asked.

"Ben, we average about 75 per day."

Ben stood up and motioned toward the whiteboard. "Mind if I do the math?"

"Sure," Steve replied.

Ben wrote on the whiteboard in Steve's office.
5 minutes for sales X 75
5 minutes for accounting X 75
30 minutes for Tia
=

As Ben started the math, Steve piped in already knowing the answer.

"780 minutes Ben."

Ben turned to Steve. "Divide by 60."

Steve's face turned red. "13 hours. 13 HOURS! Half of that wasted because of a stupid hierarchy fix."

Ben sat back down in front of Steve's desk. "Yes, Steve, 13 hours." Ben slowed his speech. "Each day!"

Steve threw his hands up. "How is this possible? Wasted time is wasted money."

"It is," Ben reassured, "but all is not lost. We can fix this."

Steve leaned toward Ben. "We have to. We are so worried about dollars we forgot about dimes and dimes is killing us. Think about not only the wasted labor cost, but the wasted opportunity costs. My accounting people, salespeople, and operations leader spend 65 hours a week on something that could be done in half that time. And I wonder why they get overtime. I am literally paying them to enter the same data over and over."

"True," Ben replied. "The difference is, you are now aware of it and can take action to fix it today."

"That I will!" said Steve with enthusiasm.

"A couple more things though before that," Ben cautioned.

"I can't wait," Steve replied with the face of a dog that was locked out all night in the pouring rain.

"Tia needs to know how much in dollars and cents inventory is on hand. And she needs two years historical data on inventory replenishment."

Steve answered, "Got it, Ben. I can have those tomorrow and will CC you."

"Lastly Steve, I noticed that some of the office spaces overlook the floor. Tia's does not; she is in a cube in the back. Can you look into moving her into one of those spaces?"

Steve looked at Ben with a bit of concern. "Ben, those offices are reserved for executives and senior leaders. I'm not sure it is a good idea to move Tia there—not sure what message it sends."

"Steve, one more thing, you told me that the cost per square foot here is 64 cents. I found the hellhole in the back loaded with a failed product. You might suggest taking a hard look at liquidating, donating, or discarding those old products. At 64 cents a square foot, I would say that inventory sitting there is costing you about $2k a month in expenses. That is space we could use to make money, not lose it because no one wants to face the truth."

"Ben," Steve replied, "what you don't understand is that we took a bath on that product and we are just trying to recover our capital outlay. We have a lot invested back there and I am hard pressed to get rid of it."

Ben replied, "Steve, are you familiar with the sunk cost fallacy? The idea that the more you invest in something, the more emotionally connected to it you get and the more likely you are to make the wrong financial decision about it?"

"Of course I am, Ben. But we have a lot invested—time, money, and labor—in that product. And to just throw it all away? I just don't see how that makes good sense."

Ben proceeded in a calm tone. "So, you'll just limp along for a few decades selling what you can and hoping for the best?"

Steve replied, "Yes, Ben, that is the strategy."

"Steve," Ben retorted, "I know you are a smart guy, but I would ask you to consider the real costs: moving those items, storing them, the space they take that could be used to improve the process, the lost revenue from potentially renting that back storage to another company. On top of that, think of the stories that people here tell every time a new hire asks about what those items are. Let's be honest, everyone who asks hears a story about how management failed. Is that really the message we want to show employees for the next decade or more?

"Think about it, Steve, all of it. I will be back in the morning at 6:45."

Ben stood up, gathered his things, and headed to the door, leaving Steve to ponder the real cost of the failed product still being such a prominent part of the business.

Steve muttered under his breath, "How can we move forward while dragging the anchor of the past?"

Chapter 7

Staples

"Good morning, everyone. Again, my name is Ben and I am here helping out and working with all of you to make this place more efficient and an overall better place to work."

Ben looked out over a large group of blue-collar workers as he proceeded.

"Yesterday, when we were together, I asked each of you to bring an accomplishment from the previous day, a goal of what you want to accomplish today, and a barrier that prohibits you from truly accomplishing something here at work."

His eyes crinkled in a smile. "Now it's time to turn in your homework."

The whole room looked worried. Many of the people looked like they didn't have a clue what was happening, so Ben let them off the hook.

"OK, OK, first day you get a pass. But I am serious. Start looking, start thinking about what you are proud of, what your goals are here, and what is stopping you. So who has something, anything, they want to share?"

A tall, dark man of 6′ 5″ or more stepped forward and held up his hand.

"My name is Raymond and I do have something. Yesterday when you talked about what we are proud of and what we want to accomplish it got me thinking. My dad used to talk that way, talking about I can do anything if I set my mind to it. It got me thinking about my job and what I do here and, as I was thinking, I realized how annoying some of this stuff is."

Susan and Steve looked concerned and some of the others in the room started shifting a bit.

"Please continue, Raymond," Ben urged.

"I don't want to be complaining or nothing, that ain't me. But I am asking why things are the way they are, and how could we make everyone's life here better. It just got me thinking, that's all. And I had a question, maybe one of them barriers you mentioned."

Raymond went on. "See, on my line we use a lot of staples to put product together. We are stapling stuff all day long. We use these big air powered staplers and, because we staple a lot, we are always refilling them. I paid attention yesterday and most of us change the staple strip every 4-5 minutes. That's a lot of staples and a lot of refilling staplers. Just wondered if there was an easier way. Something that would reduce our need to refill so much.

Maybe like," Raymond shrugged and smirked, "more staples in a strip." The group all laughed a little, but plenty of heads nodded.

Ben turned to Tia and mimed for to her to make a note.

Ben then addressed the group. "Thank you, Raymond that is really helpful, and something I promise you we will look into right away.

"See folks it's as easy as that. Replacing those strips every few minutes is not efficient, and Raymond pointing that out gives us the chance to try to fix it. I am not saying we *can* fix it. But at least we have a shot, all because Raymond pointed it out. Does that make sense?"

Lots of heads nodded up and down and Ben noticed a sidebar conversation occurring in the back.

"Folks in the back there, what is it?" A young Hispanic man stepped forward and looked over his shoulder at the others for help. Tia rushed over and said, "It's OK, I'll translate."

The young man turned to Ben and said. "My name is Julio," he then turned to Tia and continued as Tia translated.

"I work here at night, I am the janitor. Ben, you talk about things that don't make sense around here, things that are wasteful. I have something to say. Something I see here every day.

"I come in at midnight after you all leave. Me and one other helper come in and clean the offices, restrooms, and the break room. Each night when we arrive, we must disarm the security system, and each night we walk into an office and warehouse where all the lights are on. Why do we need all the lights on here when no one is here? Are we trying to make things easier for the mice?" Everyone laughed as Julio pointed to the floor as if he was tracking a mouse with is finger.

Tia continued to translate. "It seems to me the lights should be off and I should turn them on as I need them. My mama always yelled at me when I lived at home. 'You own stock in the electric company?' she would say. So, I ask you Ben, do we own stock in the electric company?"

The team laughed again. It seemed Julio was a bit of a joker, but his point was clear. Why were we wasting electricity to light the facility for no one? Ben motion to Steve to make a note.

"Thank you, Julio. Anything else?" Julio laughed under his breath and looked nervously to Tia as if to get permission to say something. Ben interrupted, "Please Julio, what is it?"

"You men pee like you are four-year-olds; none of you can aim, for nothing." Tia blushed while translating.

The team burst into laughter as both Steve and Sarah looked horrified. Ben didn't miss a step.

"Sorry, Julio, what do you mean?"

Julio continued through Tia. "The bathrooms here are a mess. No one seems to have any aim, and, in the end, I have to clean it up. It would be nice if you guys could hit the target at least sometimes."

As the laugh subsided, Ben spoke up.

"OK, folks, calm down. Thank you, Julio, for your suggestions. Steve, I am going to let you work on the first one and I will see what I can do on the last one."

Julio stepped back to his spot with a huge smile and a few pats on the back from those around him.

"OK team," Ben continued, "now you see how it's done. Something you are proud of, an accomplishment or goal for the day, and a barrier. Now let's get out there and get things done."

The group headed to the factory floor with a lot of laughter, chatter, and pats on the back for both Raymond and Julio.

Ben turned to Susan and Steve, and motioned Tia over to them.

"Well, what did you think?" Ben asked while looking to Susan.

"Interesting," Susan replied. "But impactful. Those ideas were great. All but Julio's last one."

Ben interjected, "Yes, Julio's last one. That was a first even for me. But it was honest, sincere and, if we could resolve these things, it would give them a real sense of us being on their team, caring about their needs and, in Julio's case, respecting his joke for what it really is—an acknowledgement that 'missing' really bothers him. Just think about it for a second. I bet these men don't miss at home much. But here at work, it seems like it's a problem."

Steve spoke up, "Yeah because at home their wife wouldn't tolerate it. And if they are single, they would have to clean it up."

"Right, Steve," Ben replied. "Doing that at work means they don't respect the place, or they know they are not accountable to the place. Both of which are symptoms of bigger problems."

Tia kept shifting, looking for a way to break away, and Susan looked really uncomfortable, too.

Ben continued. "OK, I see this is not a conversation we are all happy about. But the reality is, we can solve it. We can likely solve all the problems and barriers that came up today. And none of them require a huge investment. Steve, what did you think about the lights being on and Julio's question about that?"

"Well, Ben, I am a bit surprised." Steve replied. "I guess I never really thought about the lights being on when we are not here. Julio makes a great point. We are paying to light these floors and, if no one is here, why are we? I am going to call our lighting and HVAC automation company; they installed the security system and manage the software for the building. There has to be a way to program the lights to shut down after hours and even come back on at certain times for the cleaning crew."

"Tia, how about you?" Ben spoke as he motioned for Tia.

"Well," Tia replied, "the staple thing is interesting. We buy the 50 count strips as we always have. I didn't realize the line was changing those out that often. I could have never imagined they used that many staples. Let me call the supplier and see what we can do. Maybe we can get longer strips, or different guns, I'm not sure."

Ben turned to Steve and Susan. "Does Sophia have permission to resolve this challenge? She will run any purchases by me, and we will do a cost benefit analysis first. OK by you?"

Both Susan and Steve nodded their heads in agreement.

"OK," Ben said, "and I have an idea for Julio's other 'problem'."

"But, before we break, I want you all to understand the importance of this moment. It is obvious we haven't put much weight, time, or effort on the ideas of employees. I get it, most companies do not. But today was our testing ground. Only a few people spoke up, others held back, others weren't tracking what they were to do, and others probably had something they just weren't sure was the correct things to say.

"What we must do, from today, is act on all these first suggestions. Show progress; show we took them seriously, even if that means we have to do something we are unsure about or that might not make 100% sense. Today is less about the ideas and more about us showing the team we are listening and taking action.

"If we do that, by this time next week we will be on the way. And Susan will walk into that Board meeting with a big smile, some good news, and a new direction."

Tia, Susan, and Steve all shook their heads as to acknowledge the importance of acting immediately.

"Steve, I need you to call the automation company today and either get the system reprogrammed or get a technician out here to find a solution. Can you update me on the status before end of day? I would like to announce the progress on this and a projected date for resolution at our 6:45 tomorrow morning."

Steve replied in the affirmative. "Will do, Ben."

Ben turned to Tia. "Tia, I need you to call the supplier today and find out what alternatives we have. Longer strips, new guns, an automated feed system—explore all the options. Find out the pricing and schedules to make each one happen and email them to me by 2 p.m. Then you and I will jump on a call at 3 p.m. and make a course of action. We will announce that tomorrow at 6:45 to the whole team."

Tia nodded that she understood while jotting down notes in her iPad.

"Finally, Steve," Ben said, "just a reminder that Tia needs some inventory figures from you today."

Steve replied, "I'm actually on top of that. Tia now has access to the reporting platform in the Accounting system and the sales people are being trained to enter orders this morning."

"Excellent," Ben called out excitedly. "As for you, Susan, would you have some time to meet me later this morning for coffee? We need to start creating a game plan for next Friday."

"Absolutely, Ben," Susan replied. "Just come upstairs to my office when you are ready."

As Steve and Susan headed back to their offices, Tia stayed back to spend a few minutes with Ben.

"Ben, thank you for resolving the issue with the accounting system. I used the system this morning and exported the data right into a spreadsheet, sorted it, and matched it up with the job jackets that are now stored in my filing cabinet. I was done at 6:10 and found myself for the first time in a long time with nothing on my plate. So, I started drawing out the spaghetti diagram. I have the rough model and I am going to start following the flow this morning."

"That's super," Ben replied. "Don't worry about tracking everything. Just follow a few examples of common products through the system. If say you have four categories or sizes of products, follow each one twice. Then look back. If you see an anomaly, go back to that one and track it again. Find the average and you are done.

"If you feel or want to confirm that people are being honest with you on what they do and the path they follow, either stand back and pretend to be measuring something else while tracking their activity. Or, better yet, I noticed you have cameras."

"Oh, yes, loads of them," Tia replied.

"Well then, you might want to do a round of tracking just with the cameras to see if those differ from the ones you track in person."

"Great idea, Ben," Tia replied.

"I am going to head up and meet Susan for coffee. Don't forget the staples. Email me directly when you know what's happening there."

"Will do, Ben, thanks."

Ben lingered for a moment in the meeting room and pulled out his iPad, searching online for just the right thing. "Got it," he exclaimed as he made an online purchase and checked out.

Next, Ben sent an email to Steve.

·····••●•••·······

Steve,

Good meeting this morning.

I need something else from you. Over the weekend can you contract someone to come in and paint the room we have been meeting in for the stand-ups. I notice the company color is orange. How about that shade—floor to ceiling, all four walls.

Thanks,
Ben

Chapter 8

How are Sales?

Ben headed down the hall toward the front stairway. As he walked past the sales department, he heard the announcement that they would finally be entering their own orders. "About time," seemed to be the sentiment.

Ben headed up the stairs to the office of Susan. Her assistant was sitting at a large desk in the hallway. Ben checked in with him and asked him to tell her he was there.

After a few moments, Susan popped out of the office and asked Ben where he would like to go.

"How about we grab a coffee downstairs and take a walk? It's a nice day out."

"Umm, OK Ben." Susan felt a bit uneasy about Ben's idea. The factory was smack dab in the middle of an industrial area, with big trucks, trains, and the like all milling about.

As Ben poured them both a cup from the communal pot, he asked Susan a few questions.

"How long have you been at this, Susan?"

"Ten years here, five at the last place. Same industry, but family owned. That was a real treat!"

"Oh yes," Ben retorted, "I could write a whole book just on family-owned businesses." Ben stopped for a moment and made a note on his iPad.

"Susan, where do you see this business in five years?"

Ben and Susan stepped out the door to the 85-degree morning weather that Phoenix loves to serve up every summer.

"Hard to say Ben. I feel like I potentially screwed this up and right now I am focused on climbing out—just breathing."

"Well," Ben said reassuringly, "this is not the end of the road. Far from it. In just a few days, we have uncovered mountains of profits that are either being thrown out or leaking out in energy bills, lost time, and fruitless activities. We can change this place, Susan, and with not nearly the effort you are thinking it will take."

"The actions will happen. They are already happening; you are the only thing that can stand in their way. You and, of course, the board."

"I see that, Ben," Susan replied. "I am not worried about me. I am licking my wounds from a few years of a flawed strategy focused on HR improvements and driving the sales people to uncover every rotten stone to find revenue. But I am concerned about the board. They have every right to, well, you know."

"Fire you, Susan?" Ben asked.

"Yeah," was Susan's downtrodden reply.

Ben and Susan turned a corner, trying to stay in the shade of the large industrial building that surrounded them.

Ben allowed a few moments of silence then began to speak. "So then, our job is to prove to them you are the leader that can get us through this. We need to give an acknowledgement to the mess we are in and then present a thorough course of action.

"Boards are fickle things. For the most part, they want to mitigate risk. They want to keep the status quo while adding a few points here and there of growth. When things are good, they want to push to the double-digit growth numbers. When things are bad, they believe the solution is frantically cutting and cutting deep. You have a unique situation here Susan.

"You have succeeded in growing the top line. But that came at a cost to the bottom.

"We must acknowledge the good and recognize that there were consequences associated with that good. Consequences outside our control but controlled by the invisible hand of the market."

Susan nodded as if to agree with everything Ben was saying.

"When we address the difficult things with the board, we must do so with a story line that shows them how we will come out of this bigger, better, and stronger."

Susan continued nodding and asked of Ben, "What do you have in mind?"

"This old dog has some tricks left," Ben laughed. "One of them is to consider what we do well and what we struggle with."

Ben stopped them both beneath the shade of an olive tree as they spoke.

"I noticed a little something while I was in the books, Susan. It seems that one of our core products is not very profitable."

Susan immediately went into CEO mode. "Yes, Ben, the 1035B's. We know all about it. It has become a loss leader. Our clients demand it and we must meet the need for the product demand. The problem is those damn kids. I say that light heartedly, but it is the truth.

"A few younger employees that worked here about three years back saw the demand for the product. They saw how we produced it and, one day, they all quit. A few months later and The Shop popped up off Baseline Road. The Shop offered the 1035B product, but at a rate we hadn't even considered before. They specialized; they focused on one single product out of a hundred and they went to war with us. Discounts, special offers, free setup, you name it. Right now, all we can do is price-match them and hope they go under.

"They took a product we sold 10,000 sets of a week at $30 and they dropped it to $20. This caused a world of confusion and frustration from our clients, who insisted we price-match to keep that business. We did lower our price to $22, and this settled things down. Soon after, they bumped their price to $22, and we have been in a stalemate ever since. Worst was that, after the fact, we realized something."

Ben looked to Susan as if wanting her to go on.

"The damn things cost us $19.50 in Cost of Goods and Cost of Labor. Add to that overhead or, God forbid, overtime and the whole thing is a black hole of loss. We probably lose $2 a set on a good day and $4 a set on a bad one. And that was last year, before the labor rate increases and the tariffs. We need to find a lot of savings to make up for that one, Ben."

Ben shook his head and asked, "Ever wonder how they did it, how they priced you out?"

"No, I was too upset about those bastards stealing our product and knowledge, and building a competitor from it."

"I see. Have you ever thought about cutting the product altogether?" Ben inquired.

"Can't be done, Ben. Our clients like to order from us because we are a one-stop shop. Even if those bastards cut our prices a bit, in the end our customer like one invoice, one delivery, one salesperson."

Ben replied, "Susan, what if you can have that and make money on the 1035B's?"

Susan said with skepticism, "Ben, if there is a way to do it, do it. I don't care what it takes. If you have to camp out here for a week and find more efficiency, do it. I just have to stop losing on those products."

Ben quickly jotted some notes in his book and turned his attention back to Susan.

"Look, Susan, we are going to get there. We will have data this time next week. We will have improvements to show and a plan to turn this around. I promise you that. Right now, you need to immerse yourself in understanding what waste is, where it is and how to combat it."

Ben continued, "What do you see here, Susan?" Susan realized that Ben had walked her to the back of The Factory and they now stood facing the dumpsters.

"Waste," Susan replied.

"And what kind of waste?"

Susan knew there was a point and was mature enough to know that Ben was leading her, so she cut to the chase.

"I don't know, Ben, tell me."

"Physical," Ben said. "This is the representation of physical waste in your process. It's the part most people focus on, it is the most visible. Easiest to touch, feel and, at times, smell. It is the easiest to look right in the face of and address. It's important for sure. But, not as important as you think.

"Can we head back inside Susan, through the back door?"

"Sure, Ben," Susan replied.

As they stepped through the back door and back into the cooler air blowing from the factory evaporative coolers, Ben stood close beside Susan as if he was telling her a secret, while holding his hand out and pointing things out to her. "But here is where the majority of the waste is. Right here in the facility. Those things outside are discarded parts and pieces. But in here it is the wasted steps and motion; the pallet that moves twice, the extra stockpile of inventory, the overproduction 'just in case', the defects, the waiting on others for materials, the under-utilized people, the extra step because 'that is how we have always done it' and, worse, the lost capacity of this building every hour these machines don't hum."

Susan soaked it all in as if she was seeing her factory in a new light. Watching all the motion, the movement, the rushing about and, finally, for the first time asking herself the question, "Is this waste?"

Ben allowed Susan a few moments to watch the factory as it moved and breathed; the people rushing about like blood running through veins, the sounds of the machines, the beeps of the forklifts as they backed up to lift a pallet.

It was as if she was looking at the factory for the first time as a living, breathing thing. Something she needed to nurture, feed, and take care of.

Ben continued. "Susan, you likely do not remember this, but when we met for the first time again a few days ago I asked you a question. Do you remember what it was?"

"Ben, to be honest I have no idea." Ben reminded her, "I asked you a simple question—How are sales?"

Susan nodded as she remembered.

"And, Susan, do you recall your response?"

"Ben, I probably said they were great, but …"

Ben interrupted Susan mid-sentence. "But, nothing. You said sales were 'great' and that was enough for me. When you told me that sales were strong, I knew right then and there we could fix this.

"You see, business is about demand. If there is no demand for the product, then you have a serious problem. But if customers want to buy the products or services, then the problem is simply finding a way to deliver the product to them at the price they are willing to pay.

"Operational problems are fixable problems. But there is no solution for a company who customers will not buy from."

"That makes me feel somewhat better," Susan said in relief. "Sales are not the problem here. It is all the operational things that we assumed would be handled by better people and an 'economy of scale' that never materialized."

Ben shook his head, and he felt the buzzing on his smart watch as he walked Susan back to the front offices.

"Thank you, Ben," said Susan. "That was the pep talk I needed. There is a lot here to celebrate; we expanded and did it rapidly, and now we have to buckle down and make this place a well-oiled machine. So far, that seems far easier than what we have accomplished to date and, once we have done it, the sky is truly the limit."

Susan headed toward her office and Ben ducked into an open conference room to check his phone.

Chapter 9

Bullseye

Email From: Tia

Ben,

I spoke with our vendor about the staples. There is a lot here to consider.

First, it seems that the 50 count strips that we use are in high demand. Everyone in town is using them and the vendor would be thrilled if we moved to a larger strip.

Our staple guns can accommodate 250's with no modification or 500's with a new insert tray – the trays are $50 per staple gun.

The newer model staple guns can accommodate 1,000 count strips. But they are $500 per unit. We would need 25 of those.

They also have a belt-fed model that can do 5,000 count reels—but that would need additional compressors, training, a rework of our air drops, etc.

I think the last option is off the table as, when I asked Simon from the vendor what that would cost, he grunted a little and whispered to me that we don't want those. 'Too many problems,' he said.

If we go from 50 to 250, that would mean that, if we assumed the average time between refills of strips would go from 5 minutes to 25 minutes, it's a huge improvement. Add in $50 per gun and we can go to 50 minutes.

The new units sound great and would really cut our change time, but the cost is high.

By the way, the vendor asked how many 50 strips we had in stock. I told him two pallets. He offered to buy those all back at our cost. So good news is if we upgrade, we won't lose anything. He was so eager to get those back he offered to pick up and deliver whatever we like today.

Thoughts?

Tia

········•••●●●•••········

Ben replied.

From: Ben

Tia,

Part of this equation is about the Cost of Labor and the time it takes to swap out a strip.

Usually I would suggest we time the swap process, divide it times the cost of labor by minute and determine the best path. In this instance, and because we want to show the team we are listening and taking immediate action, I believe we should take the path of least resistance and take up the vendor on his offer of buying the 50's back and have him sell us a few days' worth of 250's.

Tomorrow at The Huddle you are going to readdress what the concern was from Raymond, and then hand out 250 strips to the operators. This will get their attention and let them see you as a leader that takes action. Furthermore, I only want you to get a few days' work because as part of the new 250 strip rollouts, you can now go to the team and tell them there might be an even better solution, but you need their help to prove it.

Do a time test like the one I described above with them over the next few days and get them involved. At the end of the day, you and they make the decision. If the upgrade of $50 per unit is worth the investment, will it make them faster, better, result in fewer injuries or errors. Once you and they work out the numbers, present it back to the team like this: 'Team, together we have determined the investment in the extended strip upgrade is worth the cost. From what we can tell, this additional improvement will result in an improvement of X%. Are you all comfortable with me presenting our findings to

111

management and telling them they can expect X% improvement for this investment?'

Making the team part of the decision and getting a tangible commitment to improvement will help you, them, and management make the right decision. And because they will have committed to a percentage improvement, accountability is baked right into the whole process.

Get those 250's and bring a case to tomorrow's meeting.

Ben

As Ben hit send on his email, his phone buzzed again. It was a voicemail from Steve.

Ben listened. "Ben, great news. The damn lights on-and-off feature is already in the alarm panel. It's a setting. I reprogrammed the system in under 5 minutes. Lights off 3 minutes after the alarm is set. Lights on immediately upon the front door opening.

"Better yet. The warehouse lights have a motion-sensor upgrade option. For less than $200, we can set a sensor up so that when Julio and his team are cleaning the offices, the factory floor lights are off. If they enter the factory, the lights turn on.

"Brilliant. We are estimating a $35,000 annualized savings on power usage.

"By the way, paint crew will be here Saturday. Not sure why you want it painted, but you just saved me $35k so I'd paint it myself, if need be!

"See you tomorrow. And Ben, thank you."

Ben gathered his things and headed out the front door. He had an important stop to make on the way home. One that he knew would make a big impact.

·····•••●●●••·····

"Once again, good morning everyone." Before Ben could give his usual "I'm Ben," about half the crew said "Good morning, Ben," like he was their 3rd grade teacher. Ben smiled and then continued.

"We have some great things to share this morning and, because of it, this meeting might run a little over. But before we go around, I want Steve to tell Julio the good news."

Steve stood beside Ben and told the team about the change to the security system, about the lights now being programmed and about the motion sensor. The team looked interested. Not overly excited, mind you, but hey, it's a start.

As Steve finished and stepped to the side, Ben motioned to Tia.

Tia explained the expansion of the staples from 50 to 250. Raymond beamed from ear to ear. His idea had helped, and others took notice. There were lots of pats

113

on the back, and a big round of applause for Raymond and Tia. Tia closed by telling the operators she would hand out new strips at the end of the meeting, and that she had gotten some more ideas for improvement but needed their help. Everyone nodded in agreement.

Ben cleared his throat and continued. "Yesterday, Julio pointed out a few things. One of them we have already fixed thanks to his observations. The other, well, it might be embarrassing and something we all get a laugh out of, but it does matter to Julio.

"Julio, can you please come up here?"

Julio pointed to himself as if he was receiving a Golden Globe then trotted to the front, with Tia in tow to interpret.

"Julio," Ben continued, "I got you something." Ben moved his bag and coat to reveal a big gift-wrapped box with a massive red bow. Julio looked shocked and proceeded to pick it up and shake it, much like a small child would do at Christmas. Julio continued his antics of acting as if he was weighing and shaking the box to determine what was inside, much to the joy of everyone in the room.

After a moment, Ben prompted Julio to open it. The rest of the team joined in, chanting, "Open it! Open it!" Julio obliged them all by tearing into the package reaching in to find hundreds of small items wrapped in paper. As he removed one from the box, he peeled back the paper and shouted out as if he was celebrating a goal for his team.

"Bullseye!" Julio exclaimed as he turned the small round disk to the team.

A urinal cake with a bullseye dead center in the middle caused uproarious laughter as Julio showed it to everyone, pointing out the center and yelling, "Bullseye! Bullseye!"

After what seemed like five minutes of antics from the whole room, including Raymond charging the stage while holding his fingers over his head like a bull's horns and kicking his leg like a bull pawing in the dust, things settled down.

"Thank you, Ben, thank you." Julio turned to Ben and gave him a big bear hug with tears in his eyes. Julio took his box and headed back to his space as the whole team applauded.

Ben let them settle again and said, "OK, team, time for The Huddle. Who's first?" Forty hands shot up like fireworks on the Fourth of July.

·····•••••••••·····

"Well, that was amazing!" Susan said to Ben as the team went to work. "There must have been ten great ideas in there and ten more well worth considering. And the fact that nearly everyone shared something— that was unreal."

Ben addressed the three of them that had now come together. "They see we are listening and acting on suggestions, and now the sky is the limit. The team knows you are serious, and they believe you trust them. One of the most important yet misunderstood aspects of management is that you need to trust the people that own things. If you don't, you will fail.

"You can keep this momentum. 6:45 a.m. daily Huddles run by the three of you is the touch point for a while, then start breaking the groups down into smaller sub-segments, but still occasionally bring them all together. This will keep setting the tone of the day and for the business. Asking people to bring something, pushing them to find improvement, and then celebrating and adopting those improvements with their help will continue building momentum. If you can adopt small things immediately, it will help the team understand that what they have to say matters. If you can, roll out the improvement in stages.

Ben continued, "Susan, Steve, what you don't know is that we have not yet fully implemented the real solution to Raymond's idea for increasing capacity of the staplers. Tia needs to do some analysis. She needs to get the operators to time some things, to try other things and then and only then can she make the case to you about what she needs for that investment. Yet, instead of dragging things out, instead of waiting, we came up with an interim solution that is a win for us and for the team, and now we can work with them to find the optimal solution that brings even more efficiency. Instead of them fighting us on change, they will work with us because it is all part of their idea."

Tia jumped in, "I get it, Ben. When I sent you that email, I was surprised you didn't choose the option to upgrade the staplers; it was low cost and will double the impact. But I get it now. Instead of one win, we will get two and along the way we will engage the team in making sure it is the right one."

"Exactly, Tia. Listen, I get it that many of your people are blue collar. They are not knowledge workers by nature or training. But getting them to engage even 1% of their time just five minutes a day thinking about improvement will make an incredible impact."

Susan piped in, "I see that now. In the past, we thought about the team out here as an engine that runs the machine. Now I see that there is so much more potential here. So many ideas. So much energy. The least we can do is listen and adopt."

Ben nodded in agreement. "When changing a culture, it is important to change everything they see and the words they hear; everything they believe to be true needs to be dismantled and put back together. A week ago, this team believed that this place would never change. Today, they believe it can change. You need to keep reinforcing that. Show them things are different, and they will act differently."

"Ben," Steve questioned, "is that why you asked me to have this entire room repainted in the company orange? So that the employees next week would be looking at something fresh and new?"

"You caught me, Steve. That is exactly the point. The hardest part about change is to believe in it when nothing has changed. Sure, the staples are important, the urinal cakes serve a purpose but, in the end, it is about changing what the team believes, what they see, how you reward them. The more that you change, the more that they will."

Chapter 10

Those "bastards"

"Good morning, I'm Ben." Ben directed his voice to the man behind the counter as the jingle of the entry doorbell subsided behind him. "Good morning, Ben, I'm Kristoff. How can I help you today?"

"I heard you guys are the best in town at producing a product I need. I believe the industry term is the 1035B."

Kristoff perked up. "Ah, yes, we *are* the best in town. Best prices, service, and quality. We built this business on that product and it is 95% of what we do. Ben, you have come to the right place. What size order are you looking for and what are your specifications?"

"Well, to be honest, I have an assortment of colors and some trim sizes for a number of brands. Just curious if you think you might be able to handle an account of our size?"

"We certainly can, Ben," Kristoff said with enthusiasm. "What do you think your monthly set count would be?"

Ben replied, "Somewhere around ten thousand units each week."

"Ten thousand a week?" Kristoff said as he choked on his words. "Come on, Ben, no one in town has a demand for that."

"No one?" Ben replied.

"Well, I take that back, there is another shop we compete with; those guys do high volume. But Ben, it's lower quality and we match or beat any price they offer. Furthermore, we specialize in this sort of thing; we have our own proprietary process and system. Our attention to detail, delivery time, and service are unbeatable."

"I agree, completely," Ben replied. "I work with Susan over at The Factory and I have a proposition for you."

Before Ben could say another word, Kristoff blurted out, "Sorry, if you guys want to fix prices or something, we are out."

"No, no, nothing like that," Ben retorted. "On the contrary, I am hoping that we can come to find common ground and partner together. I told you the truth from the beginning. We are producing over ten thousand sets of 1035B each week and, candidly, your pricing, your quality, your delivery is… well, I am not going to say it out loud." Ben smirked and so did Kristoff.

Ben went on. "Would you agree that you are exceptional at this product? And we are exceptional at many other things?" Kristoff nodded, albeit reluctantly. "I came here today to see if you might consider an arrangement where we become your customer."

Kristoff looked intrigued. "Please go on, Ben."

"My thought is that we pass all orders for 1035B's on to you for production. You then ship those products to our customers on our behalf. The customer would only see our name, but you would do the production and fulfillment. In turn, we—you and I—would negotiate a fair price, one that has margin in it for you, but one we can also live with, both parties taking into consideration what the other one has to do. In essence, you have to produce a high-quality product, quickly, and we have to pay you promptly, invoice the customers, collect from the customers, and take the orders."

"Ben, that all sounds well and good but I am not sure my machines can handle the extra volume. I mean, you are talking about us producing three times what we usually do in a month. I guess I could add an extra shift, but even still—I would need a capital infusion to buy another machine, maybe two."

"Kristoff, didn't you used to work at The Factory?"

"Yes, I did," Kristoff replied.

Ben continued, "What type of machines do we use?"

"The same type," Kristoff replied. "But yours are a little newer."

"So what if," Ben suggested, "we sold you those machines as part of the arrangement? We all agree to a fair market value, bump it up by, say, 15% as a surcharge for then giving you 24 monthly payments."

"That would be incredible, Ben. Do you really thing Susan would be open to this?"

"I believe she might Kristoff, if the terms were right."

"OK, Ben, since we are being straight here, the truth is we do 1035B's exceptionally well. We have three other products we also are producing, but we are losing our shirts on those. I know Susan has the capacity to do more of those. Could we do the same thing, but in reverse—we stop doing them completely and send them to you? We bill our customer, mark up your cost to us, and you fulfill on our behalf?"

"Sounds reasonable," Ben replied.

Kristoff thought for a moment and then continued. "There may be another opportunity here as well. I have a request for a proposal on my desk from an old college buddy. He is the CEO of a big firm now and would like us to produce his 1035B's for him. I jumped at the chance, but in filling out the proposal, I discovered they pay in 60-day terms, no less. Frankly, Ben, I don't have the cash flow to support that kind of float. I'd run myself straight out of business. I know I can get the contract, I know we will kill it on the quality, but I will have to pass on this deal because I can't make the money work."

Ben could see where this was going and interjected, "So, you submit the proposal in collaboration with us. We do the billing, we float the terms and pay you on the terms you need, and we mark up the work for the trouble."

"Bingo!" Kristoff shouted. "We both win. I get the business and the terms I need, you float the invoice and get the markup."

"Sounds promising, Kristoff," Ben replied. "But we need to ask fast. Next Friday, I have our board in town and we would need a Memo of Understanding with all the terms and prices written up for their blessing. When is the soonest you could get me pricing for that kind of volume of 1035B?"

"Ben, I can have that for you this afternoon."

"Excellent," Ben responded. "I will have an independent assessor come in and value the machines we will sell to you. Is there someone you would recommend?"

Kristoff replied, "I am comfortable with Tony down at Ash Street Machine. He works in our industry and, although I might not always like his assessment, I know he is fair and both of us will agree to whatever Tony says."

"OK, Kristoff, I am on that. I will also get you a wholesale price structure from us. I would think we would just offer you a blanket discount. That way, if you have a customer that wants a product, you can easily offer it to them.

Ben looked directly at Kristoff to see if he would flinch. "We will also have to agree not to poach customers from each other."

Kristoff jumped in, "We are in this together, Ben. It's not worth risking the opportunity for a measly account."

"Agreed," Ben replied enthusiastically. "As for the request for proposal, when do you need to submit that?"

"Today! They want to decide who they are going with by 5 p.m. tomorrow. Ben, would it be OK to go ahead and submit it to them under the assumption we will do business together? I guess, worst case, I may have to hand it off to you, regardless."

Ben acknowledged, "Do it. Submit it today. We will get this done."

"Alright, Ben," Kristoff replied. "I will start making calls right now to determine my best price for you on the 1035B's at that volume. I'll text you a number after lunch."

Ben reached out his hand to Kristoff. "I am excited about where this is going."

"Me too, Ben, me too!"

Ben headed back out the door and decided he had been missing his "office" all week.

· · · · · • • ● ● ● • • · · · · ·

"Good morning, Ben!" Came a choir of voices from all over The Diner. Ben headed over to his favorite spot and was met table-side with his usual—black coffee.

"Anything else today, Ben, or are you working?" questioned the waitress.

"Working today, Anna, thanks."

"OK, Ben, holler if you need anything," Anna replied as she walked away from the table.

Ben opened his laptop and began drafting the MOU.

> *This Memo of Understanding is between The Factory and The Shop and was agreed upon ...*

Ben continued typing away, but a text message alert buzzing his smart watch interrupted him.

"$17 apiece. Thanks, Ben," was the message. Ben knew exactly what it was, and it was good news.

Ben looked back to his notes from his conversation with Susan about the 1035B's.

"$19.50." Ben uttered to himself. "And that was before overhead! Susan expected those products to sell at a $2 loss. Now, selling that product for exactly the same price while no longer doing the work makes us $5 to $7 per set in our favor."

Ben pulled out his phone and texted Susan. "You available in an hour?"

"Yes," Susan replied.

Ben finished the MOU, adding in the details, but leaving the price of the machines as "To Be Determined by Ash Street Machine and sold to The Shop at a 15% premium in exchange for 24 equal monthly payments."

Ben included nothing about the deal Kristoff had mentioned. "No need to muddy the water with something that isn't inked," Ben thought to himself.

After a single refill and paying the bill, Ben headed out the door toward The Factory.

$$\cdots\cdots\bullet\bullet\bullet\bullet\bullet\bullet\bullet\bullet\cdots\cdots$$

Ben walked into Susan's office and sat down.

"Susan, I have good news."

Ben slide the MOU across the table. Susan removed her glasses from their rhinestone case and placed them on her face.

"Oh, Ben, The Shop?" Susan reacted with a disgusted tone.

"Read on," Ben replied.

Susan read on, continuing to utter 'hmm' sounds starting with a deep grunt of disgust and slowly building into a sound that was like a cat purring.

Susan put her glasses down, took a breath, and looked at Ben. "Ben, these terms are good. Fair. Equitable. But

I just can't get over partnering with 'them,' after what they did. If it was anyone but 'them', I would be thrilled. Keep the revenue, sell the equipment, stop worrying about how to make it profitable—and the immediate bump to margin would be a Godsend, from the red to the black with a stroke of a pen. But, Ben?"

Ben leaned forward toward Susan. "Susan, may I tell you a story?"

Ben didn't wait for the answer, he began.

"Long ago, a farmer had a prized horse. It was the fastest most beautiful horse in the land. One day the horse ran away, and a neighbor stopped to offer his condolences. 'I am sorry for this great loss' the neighbor said. The farmer replied, 'Who knows what is good or bad?' The neighbor walked away confused. 'Of course this is bad,' he thought. 'What good could come of it?'

"The next day, the horse returned followed by twelve feral horses. The neighbor saw this and said to the farmer, 'Congratulations on your great fortune, you are a very lucky man that such good would befall you.' The farmer replied, 'Who knows what is good or bad?'

"The next day the farmer's son was trying to tame one of the horses, was thrown, and broke his leg. The neighbor came by and said, 'I am sorry about your son.' The farmer replied…" Ben pointed to Susan to allow her to say the words herself.

"Who knows what is good or bad?" Susan responded.

Ben continued, "The next day, the King and his army marched on the village to conscript all the able-bodied young men to fight in a great war across the sea, but the farmer's son couldn't go because of his broken leg.

"Susan?" Ben again pointed to Susan. Susan repeated, "Who knows what is good or bad?"

"In this situation you feel wronged. Even when faced with a major piece of your own solution, you are still holding on to what you feel was badly done to you. Even when that thing has the potential to be of great good to you. You see, Susan, 'who knows what is good or bad?'

"This situation, which you saw as bad, might be the one thing that saves us. How many times in life does something good turn out to be bad and something bad turn out to be good?"

Susan nodded her head, reached for her glasses, lifted her pen and, in under a second, turned the page to a new chapter.

Ben shook his head in affirmation. He removed the MOU from Susan's desk, took his things and left without saying a word.

Chapter 11
Tia

Tia opened her iPad to review her notes and assess her work in progress and the items she had completed.

"Based on the data accounting sent to me," Tia thought, "I have been able to figure out how quickly we use items in inventory. From that, I know how much I have on hand and how quickly we can get those items. From that, I was able to determine the number of days of inventory and setup my ordering schedule based upon getting materials coming 'Just in Time'. Instead of truckloads of inventory we pay for today but don't use for weeks or months, we now negotiate based upon our annual spend with a vendor, then parse out delivery as needed.

"I have been able to think about activities done at work as two categories; work and waste. Whatever is adding value to the client is work, everything else is waste. I trained the line leads on this concept, and now we scrutinize everything we do, and we ourselves and each other what category if falls into." Tia verbalized this last bit. "The items that are waste, we address with the tools Ben has given us; the items that are work, we reinforce."

Tia pulled out two large 11x17 pencil drawings of the facility with a bunch of colored lines all over it, and on her iPad she pulled up an Excel spreadsheet she had created.

Tia thought to herself, "Ben had me draw out the whole production facility and then follow our operators and leads around to see where they went all day. I tracked their steps and measured out how far they walked with a rolling measure. It's a digital measuring device that has a handle on it so you can just walk and get a measurement as you roll along. I tracked the feet our people moved and the feet our materials moved.

"I then drew colored lines on that diagram of the whole facility showing where each person and material came from and went to. There is a lot of waste. This one lead walked nearly 30,000 steps each day to get materials for his line!

"The standard size base material for about 65% of our products was located an average of 339 feet from the lines and my leads would go pull the material 4-5 times each day, for each line.

"After I did all the counts on how many feet the materials and we moved, I created another diagram, this time moving the machines, people, and inventory around to find the best, most efficient path. Ben helped me get others involved and share their ideas and suggestions. Within a couple days, we had a new layout and, get this, Sophia—we had a 67% decrease in the distance materials travelled and a 49% decrease in the feet people walked each day! All told, as a team each day, we walked the equivalent of two marathons! Ten marathons a week."

Tia crafted an email to Ben showing all the improvements the move would make

From Tia:

Ben,

Attached is the spreadsheet. The changes are substantial. For the most part, the costs to implement this plan are associated with the movement of 10 electrical drops, the re-routing of four air drops and the labor associated with moving the lines and removing some of the excess pallet racking in order to accommodate the shift of the lines to allow inventory to be staged there.

Costs are as follows.

$2,000 for the electrical
$800 for the air lines
$1,450 for the racking company to come and tear down those racks. IF we no longer need or want those racks, they will purchase them for $2,965.

I will have to schedule some of our people to work the weekend to help with the move. I am going to estimate 100 hours in labor (but keep in mind, that is all Overtime.) Taking the average of our blended hourly rate and adding in the OT costs we will spend $2,500 on labor.

All in all, $6,750 and if we want to sell the racking back to the racking company for $2,965, we are at $4,250 total cost to us.

This gets us a decrease in the steps people take by 49% and reduces the distance that material travels by 67%.

Seems to me we need to pull the trigger immediately.

Tia

················•••●●●••••········

From Ben:

Tia,

I agree, let's get this scheduled and tell the racking company we will sell the racks back to them.

Add a line item in your budget for $1,750 for materials, bringing us to $6,000 even.

First, if we are asking the team to work all weekend, we want to reward them with donuts for breakfast, something for lunch and let's see if we can get an ice cream truck as a late afternoon treat. Can you call around on that and check the cost?

We also need some other materials and I can order those. First, we need some directional floor stickers—this will tell people the direction of the aisles. We will also need colored tape, lots of it. We want to mark out all the aisles; we need to create areas for everything by marking out on the warehouse floor where everything goes—pallet jacks, garbage cans, walkways, recycling bins, etc.—everyone will always know where everything goes, and the place will stay neat and tidy. When we mark off where everything belongs, it also creates a way for the activities on the floor to be either self-managed or patrolled by everyone. If John doesn't put the pallet jack back in its place after he uses it, everyone can see the jack is out of place and remind him to comply.

When there is a place for everything, the company and people save both time and frustration. Any time spent looking for something is waste.

Great work, Tia. Let's get this move scheduled starting Friday after work and completing by 6:30 a.m. Monday morning.

Ben

·······•••◉•••·······

"Good morning, Tia," Ben exclaimed as he entered Tia's new office. "Nice office you have here."

Tia's desk was facing a large blank wall and to her right was her view of the factory floor.

"Yes, I love it," Tia replied. "I feel like I have more control on what is happening now. Steve pulled some strings to get me this spot. And check this out." Tia motioned for Ben to turn around so that he could see the 65-inch TV mounted on the wall to the left of her desk, showing a live stream of all camera feeds.

"Originally, the installer wanted to mount it here," Tia pointed to the large blank wall directly in front of her desk. "But I insisted it be mounted here."

Ben questioned, "I see that, but why here and not directly in front of you."

"Well," Tia continued, "I felt that me being able to the see the camera feed was secondary to the people on the floor being able to see that I had a screen, with all the feeds on it, in my office. As you put it Ben, people only respect what you inspect. I knew that, over time, the screen would become background for me. But for the team, every time they look toward the offices, they are reminded I—no, we—are paying attention."

"Good idea, Tia."

"Thanks, Ben!" Tia continued. "So, what can I do for you?"

"Just checking," Ben replied. "Wanted to make sure you were on track. The big board meeting is this Friday and I want to make sure that everything this weekend goes off without a hitch. Can you give me an update on the status of everything?"

"Sure," Tia replied. "It'll be good to have an extra set of eyes on this as well."

Tia pulled out a printout outlining the activities, schedule, job assignments, and order in which things would be moved and placed.

"First and foremost, Ben, I need to get these drops moved. I have calls in to our electricians, as I found they can do both the air and electrical drops. They are to be here at 4 p.m. on Friday, to begin moving the power and air as we are moving machinery."

"Excellent," Ben replied. "One suggestion—bring lots of copies of the layout, plan, and schedule. Then one day, either before everyone gets here or after they leave, take some tape out on the floor and mark off exactly where the drops and air should be. An X marks the spot in different colors for each would be helpful.

"And," Ben continued, "it just dawned on me that you might not have heard about The Shop arrangement!"

"Ben, we are on it! Steve and I spoke after The Huddle this morning and I reworked the floor plan to accommodate the moving out of that equipment. The owner of The Shop is coming by today to coordinate the pickup and setup on their end."

Chapter 12
Steve & Susan

Ben slid into his regular both and the waitress immediately greeted him with his morning coffee. "Anything else, Ben?" she asked. "Nope, I am good." was the reply.

Ben opened his iPad and began jotting down notes about The Factory progress, notes he would use to create a summary report for the executive team and board.

Steve found that 1% overruns should be the new standard. A digital counter was placed on each machine. The downstream operators would pull aside anything outside the deviation and share it with Tia. Tia would then work back through the process to find out where the problem originated and resolve it immediately.

The overrun number was improving each day and, as a byproduct of the operator' greater attention to the counts, the quality was improving as the rework rates were falling. Rework that was previously the result of people not paying attention was being eradicated in every aspect of the business as people were paying closer attention to the procedures and sharing their success and barriers.

Furthermore, the waste of Defects was falling quickly as well. More attention to the processes and materials resulted in a higher quality of work and less mistakes. When the operators were conscious of what was happening, and when management was inspecting the process and the outcome of it, the operators took more pride in the work.

Some defects were found to be the result of inconsistent material quality. In one instance, Steve requested samples from other vendors and found their material was higher quality. After ordering a small amount and going down to the line to run it through the machines with the operators, it was decided that this new material would work better. It did require some machine adjustments, as the weight of the material was a slightly more than the former material, but within two shifts the change was made and quality improved.

In another instance, Steve requested samples from competitors. After nearly an hour working with the material with the operators, it was found that the existing supplier was providing the highest quality available. Steve contacted the vendor and explained that the product was resulting in a higher than normal number of reruns versus other products The Factory produced. Steve sent the company the analysis that showed .5% failure rate with their product dating back for the last year and the company immediately credited The Factory for the .5% defects, resulting in a credit of $14,500. The vendor assured Steve that they would look into improving the quality of the material and asked if he could provide them this report each month so they could use the data to improve.

Ben closed his iPad and took a long drink of coffee from his cup. While pondering the impacts of all the improvement. He then packed his things and headed for The Factory.

·····•••●●•••······

"Welcome, Kristoff," Susan said as she extended her hand. "Nice to see you again. I am really excited about this partnership."'

Ben also outstretched his hand and Kristoff one-upped him and pulled him in for a hug. Ben's not a big fan of hugs, but in this instance, well, he guessed it made sense.

"So am I, Susan," Kristoff replied. "Glad we were able to come to an agreement that benefits us both. And so glad there are no hard feelings."

"You know, Kristoff," Susan replied, "I have recently come to the conclusion to not assume something is good or bad, but to look at things as they are and see where it leads. To be honest, this leads us both down a path that neither of us could have traveled alone. I have the agreement here with my signature. We just need you to sign the copies as well."

Kristoff picked up the pen off Susan's desk and signed both copies.

Kristoff immediately looked at Susan and Ben, and said, "In addition to the new relationship, I am happy to say that I received an email this morning which says we have received a $500,000 annual contract with a new client."

"Good for you!" Susan exclaimed.

Ben jumped in, "Good for all of us, Susan. In the spirit of cooperation, Kristoff and I worked on this deal together. Kristoff needed our equipment and our terms to be able to service the client while he fulfills the work. We have agreed that we will handle customer service and extend terms to the customer while paying Kristoff in a fashion that allows him to keep his cash flow under control. Our part of the agreement gives us a 12% margin for our trouble."

"That IS great news!" Susan replied. "This is truly a partnership."

"It is," replied Kristoff. "Do you both have a few moments to discuss some logistics on the new relationship?"

"Of course!" Susan replied.

"I have a truck and installer scheduled for Saturday morning, and I just confirmed with Tia that those machines will be the first thing disconnected and moved to the loading dock Friday night so my guys can pick up and install over the weekend. That way, on Monday, we are up and running.

"I'm also meeting with Steve right after this to talk about the hand-off of orders, since as of Friday at 4 p.m. you will no longer be producing the products we will handle. We will need to start setting up orders on Wednesday so they can be on the machine first thing Monday."

"All that sounds good, Kristoff," Ben replied. "Anything else we can do to help?"

"I hate to ask, but if there is any chance you can send your operators of those machines over on Monday morning first thing? We would love for them to walk us through. I know I used to operate one of them, but it would be safer for us all if your team came over and made sure we are squared away."

Ben replied, "I'll text Tia now and make sure those operators report to The Shop at 6:45 a.m. Monday."

Kristoff continued, "Another thing, and I don't want this to come off the wrong way, so please accept this in the spirit of the partnership.

"Back when I and my partners worked here, we noticed that there was a flaw in your system. Your sales reps are very eager, and many times would place orders that did not include all the pertinent details—colors, sizes, graphics, etc. Because there was a lot of pressure to get things scheduled and billed, many times—like, more than a quarter of the time—work orders made it to the floor that did not have the pertinent information. If that was a graphic, generally we would hold that order on the side and then the line lead or Tia would chase down the details. If it was a question of size or color, we would usually hold

141

that job jacket for a day or two. But, if we got no answer, we would guess on those elements to move the job off our plates. Many times, we guessed correctly. If a customer always used Perfect Blue for their print, we pretty much could assume that Perfect Blue was the color. But we weren't always right, and when we weren't, we had to rework the whole project from start to finish."

Ben chimed in, "Why do we allow projects to be scheduled that we don't have the details for?"

Kristoff continued, "From the factory floor perspective it always felt like every job was a rush, and if we didn't at least get it scheduled and started, we might lose the business. Or, at least, that is what the sales team led us to believe.

"We always operated in a state of waiting then rushing. That rushing caused mistakes and accidents, so we as a group tried to anticipate what we were waiting for and then produced it in the hopes we were right.

"This information was never addressed. Every day we got our job jackets and every day we tried to manage the ones we were waiting on. We were always trying to move things through even if they were incomplete in order to avoid a backup."

Kristoff continued, "I want to bring it up because this challenge was one of the reasons we left and felt there was an opportunity to do these products better, faster, and cheaper. Because of that, we are very diligent with what we will start producing and what we cannot start.

142

"For this partnership to work, we can only accept orders once all elements of art, color, size, etc. are received. We can't afford to start and stop projects or assume what the customer wants. Ben, over the last week I read your book <u>Playbook for Frontline Managers</u> and I kept thinking about the way you break down 'assume—it makes an ass of you and me.'

"We want this to work, and need to keep the process tight for it to work and for us to maintain the costs we have."

Susan thanked Kristoff, assuring him that The Factory would tighten the process and there would be no waiting in the relationship between The Factory and The Shop.

Both parties left in agreement and, as Kristoff left Susan's office, Ben and Susan stayed behind.

Ben spoke first. "Was that a surprise, Susan?"

"Ben, I want to say Yes, but it isn't. We have heard from the floor for years that we had a problem with the way we allowed customers to send us parts and pieces of a project yet still feel that we are obligated to turn the product quickly.

"I suppose I allowed it because I didn't want to upset customers, but it seems I upset my employees and wreaked havoc on my bottom-line. Waiting turned into defects and wasted motions, which resulted in over-production that caused rework. Rework created overtime and, with margins being so tight—or even non-existent for the 1035B's—that resulted in us doubling down on both Cost of Goods and Cost of Labor, doubling the losses right down the line."

Ben nodded in agreement, as Susan continued.

"A leaky fishbowl that we tried to correct by adding more water and trying to upgrade our people. When all the while the problem was our process. What were we thinking?"

Ben replied, "You were thinking that the management gurus had it all together. You were thinking that offense is the only way to win. Of course, you have to have a strong offense. Sales, marketing, customer service, production, etc. But you almost MUST," Ben said in a tone of righteous anger, "spend considerable time on your defensive strategy. Companies that don't have a part of their management team or staff dedicated to defense will do OK when they have the ball: a strong economy, high demand, a government subsidy, or a unique foothold on a market position. But, in the long run, playing defense is the only way to survive and prosper, both in the times of plenty or in coming times of lean."

Ben continued, "The approach we have been taking for the last week has been defensive. Protect the 'ball'." Ben held up his fingers in air quotes. "We must continue that and also add to it. Dedicating a part of your day to defense, hiring a Chief Process Officer or a number of process-oriented people that can constantly coach the improvement process will help immensely. Develop your people to be the eyes and ears of the company.

144

Encourage them to point out inconsistency or waste. Keep doing The Huddles, The Walkabout, etc. These are all defensive tools. They are tools that allow you to inspect the areas where leaks are happening."

"All waste is lost profits. I think as you and your team have been seeing waste as something that resides in the dumpster, but it is so much more than that. It is everywhere; every process unattended, every motion unobserved, every metric not questioned.

Susan nodded, "I see it now Ben, we can't swing the pendulum the whole way to defense. But, if we have no defensive strategy and staff, we are opening ourselves up to substantial risk, not just from the market turning but from competitors that exist or that we create. Just look at The Shop. Kristoff worked here and saw the flaws; they were so big he was able to see that there was an opportunity. Reality is, had we been listening we likely could have capitalized on the opportunity. Instead, we got taken to the woodshed.

"I'll speak with Steve and incorporate some staff in our hiring plan that are fully 100% focused on our process, both improving and sustaining it."

········•••●●●•••········

In the days leading up to Friday's board meeting, things improved daily.

Each day, The Huddles got better. Some days were better than others, but each day they were better than the day before; ideas, suggestions, commitments to improve, things to celebrate.

The lights now worked just like Steve scheduled them. And Julio was pleased—the guys in the shop were now hitting the "target" more like adults than children.

Each day, Susan, Steve, and Tia walked the floor separately and each day they discovered more and more. The more they inspected, the more people respected.

Tia and Ben submitted her plan for improvement of the shop floor and the expense was approved on the spot. Tia had been spending the week making sure everyone knew what was coming, and she was shocked at how many people wanted to help.

Susan worked on the presentation for the Board and was excited by all the new energy.

The team loved the Orange Breakroom and saw it for what it was—a new chapter.

Chapter 13

The Board Meeting

Ben and Steve stepped through the door as Susan's assistant guided them to the conference room adjacent to Susan's office. Twelve Board members, including Susan, sat around a long oval table. Ben and Steve's eyes took a moment to adjust to the surprise of the new boardroom paint job. Bright orange, just like the meeting room. Susan nodded to them both with a smile.

Susan stood up as Ben and Steve settled in their chairs. "Members of the Board, we are here today to discuss our successes and challenges of these last quarters, and to set forth the course of action for the future.

"First, I want to give you an update on where our strategy of rapid growth and hiring better people has gotten us. Then I will address the challenges this has created and present to you the plan and roadmap we will use for the near future in order to take the success we have had from a sales side and translate that into bottom-line growth.

"Before I begin, I want to introduce the new face in the room; a face that is new to this board room but likely familiar to many of you. Ben here has been helping us better determine our strategy for growing our margins and improving our profit performance."

As Susan spoke, more than half the members around the table acknowledged Ben, having worked with him in the past, attended his workshops, or read his work.

Susan continued, "As you likely have all seen from the financials that I distributed yesterday morning to you each via email, our top line revenue performance is again at record levels. Sales have been growing exponentially, and our pipeline and projections show that growth continuing into the foreseeable future.

"The challenge, as you have all become aware, is the bottom line. Increased pressure on price, rising Costs of Goods, a strong labor market that has required us to increase wages, and the now-implemented and forthcoming tariffs have affected our margins.

"Our strategy for this year was sell, sell, sell and hire better people. We have done both with great success. In retrospect, though, these strategies had a negative effect on profits.

"Higher wages and costs deteriorated our margin. The better people we hired came at a higher cost, and the increase in productivity never materialized."

Nazem, one of the younger members of the board, a man who had sold his successful manufacturing business a few years back, piped in. "Susan, we can see that the effect was not what was anticipated. But what about the economies of scale here? Producing more orders should have made us more efficient, and more volume with vendors should translate into better margins. Have they not?"

"Unfortunately," Susan replied, "they did not. The increases all around have eaten up the margins and the new, more expensive hires performed no better. The increase in sales translated into more overtime for our older workers and new ones alike, and when we tried to push the employees to take the overtime shifts, we got push-back. They didn't want the hours. The only people that would take the hours were our more experienced laborers, ones that had been here for 10 plus years and were at the highest possible end of the pay scale."

Another board member, George, interrupted. "Back in my day, people fought over OT. Everyone wanted it for extra spending cash. They relied on the OT money. What changed?"

Steve jumped in. "George, you would be surprised. Take a guess at what percent of our labor force drives for Uber or Lyft, charges Bird Scooters, delivers for Amazon, or shops for people via Instacart?"

George replied, "To be honest, I have no idea."

"36% of all Americans have a side job like one of these, according to a 2018 Gallup Poll. Here at The Factory, I would say we are closer to 50%. And, coming into Christmas, it's much higher than that. People like these 'side hustle' gigs because they give them more autonomy and flexibility."

George and the others nodded, knowing many people that had been doing these kinds of jobs; some for a primary source of income, others for fun and enjoyment.

Steve continued. "It's tough. We are in a market where labor is hard to find and expensive to keep. For the most part, once they turn 40, they are out. Overtime is not a thing they are particularly interested in and, if we demand it, well, they might just move on."

"Thank you, Steve, for that data." Susan took command of the room. "Let's talk about the plan.

"Sales continue to be strong, but truth be told, our people haven't done a great job at pricing. It has come to our attention that we are discounting or not charging for some services as much as we should be. The sales reps were told to make it rain, and they did. But in some cases, the rain is not profitable. Steve and I have gotten a better grip on the sales team and we have changed some policies and systems that were allowing these giveaways to go under-reported. The problem is resolved, and the results of the change will start to come through in Q3."

Nazem spoke up. "Excuse me, Susan. I know the 1035B issue has been a constant pain in the neck. Do we have a solution here?"

"Yes!" replied Susan. "I will address that in a moment."

The whole board looked relieved.

Susan continued. "We also have taken a hard look at our operations and recognized that we have significant inefficiencies to address. We have broken these into eight distinct categories and Steve, Tia, who is our Ops

Director, and I will address each one accordingly with the help of Ben.

"If you look on at your printed report you will see a list of the eight items we will focus on:

> Transportation,
> Inventory,
> Motion,
> Waiting,
> Over-production,
> Over-processing,
> Defects, and
> Under-utilized Skills

"We have already started on the list and are making huge strides. On Inventory we are moving to Just in Time. Steve has a report at the end of the presentation which shows how that improves our cash flow.

"With Transportation, Tia has completed a spaghetti diagram of a new, optimized layout that would reduce the steps we walk on the factory floor on a daily basis by nearly 50%. That changeover will begin at 4 p.m. this evening, and will be completed on Monday by 6:30 a.m.

"Over Production is another area where we already have tangible results to present. In the process of our Walkabouts with Ben, we found that our operators were over-producing inventory under the dated belief that our cutters would have a high number of errors. We have run an analysis with the newer machinery and discovered that we can reduce the current rates of over production by close to 80%. This in and of itself will add an estimated 1.5% to our bottom line. On top of that, we discovered that some of the materials we were sourcing caused an abnormal level of defects. After shopping for an alternative, we learned that all vendors of this product struggle with quality. We decided to keep our current vendor and they will credit us for defective material.

"With Skills, we are addressing this on both ends. Primarily, better people did not solve the problems of operations. Therefore, we are going back to our old hiring policy and will be more lenient with our hiring process. Ben rightly identified that our processes were not defined clearly. Because of that, we were depending on better people to be the solution when the real solution is better systems and more defined, published, and dynamic processes that allow people to provide feedback and suggestions. Add to that a different, more nimble approach to processes, and we feel we have a solid handle on things.

"We have and will continue to combat each of these areas, and we are already seeing the interconnectedness of one area having a deep effect on other areas.

"On the other side of the Skills challenge we have inspired our people to help us improve by asking them directly, every day, for their ideas and suggestions, as well as what barriers they see in their path."

A few of the Board members shifted about uncomfortably.

152

Susan kept going, "Now, I know what some of you are thinking. What kind of ideas are our people going to give us, what kinds of issues will they bring up? What will all this cost and what if we don't implement the ideas—will that discourage the employees?

"All good questions and all resolved through Ben's approach. Ben, would you mind explaining?"

"Sure, Susan. Thanks for having me here today. For the most part, the reason that management doesn't solicit ideas from employees on the front line is either that we expect those ideas to be not be good or, if they are, too difficult to implement. Sure, an idea about automation could be a good one and have an impact, but the cost of automating might not be worth the investment."

Ben continued, "So we limit the ideas that people bring by asking them for ideas that improve whatever they are working on by just 1%."

George chimed in again. "1% isn't much, Ben."

"George, you are right," Ben replied. "1% is very little, 1% is easy. Who can't find 1%?"

The heads around the room nodded.

"But," Ben continued, "1% each day over the course of a year is over 3,800%."

Ben let that one hang in the air for a bit before he continued.

"Even if your people fail miserably at 1% better each day and get half of that, you'll still see a massive transformation. Even if your people only get it right 10% of the time, your business will be on a trajectory it never has been on before.

"1% limits the ideas, it limits the focus, and it makes it so easy and attainable that everyone believes they can do it. Instead of asking for big ideas, ask for little ones, but ask for them every day."

George shook his head and acknowledged, "That's a damn good idea, Ben, a damn good one. No big projects or overhauls, just good old fashion do-it-better-today-than-the-day-before. I like it!"

Ben replied, "That is not to say there isn't a time or place for big ideas, it's just that big ideas can be incredibly disruptive. Little ones are easy and little ones add up to more than the big ones do, over time."

Susan lets the nods subside before she continued. "On to the question of the 1035B's and what we do about them. Starting next Monday, we are in partnership with The Shop. They do it better, they do it faster, and we have been able to negotiate a deal that will take 1035B's from a loss leader to one of our most profitable products. Better still, The Shop will fulfill orders under our name so our customers will never see any change to their relationship with us. We handle customer service, billing, and sales; The Shop produces and fulfills.

"As for the machines we have to run the 1035B product, we have sold them on installment payments to The Shop so they can fulfill our demands.

"Thanks to Ben," Susan continued, "1035B is no longer a stone around our neck."

The board applauded. The solution to the problem had been resolved and would no longer be an issue discussed each Board Meeting.

Susan continued, "Members of the Board, I believe you can see that we have a well-thought out plan. One that is already in action. Yes, the last two quarters have been challenging, but as you can see from Steve's financial summary, the wheels are in motion for Q3 and Q4 to be our best ever. Shedding the burden of low margin products, capturing more of our billing, reducing over production and the number of steps people take each day are critical to our success. And reducing the inventory burden also means our cash flow is increasing each day.

"Instead of a focus on better people, we will focus on a better process, so we need less skilled people and a lower headcount. Let's make our process world class so our people will be world class.

"But in addition to all these moves in the right direction, I also want to address with you some more strategic issues that Ben and I have been working on behind the scenes. Ben, would you like to continue?"

Ben stood. "Certainly, Susan." Ben turned to the Board. "As many of you know, I am systems guy. I love processes and I love tools that help managers manage more efficiently. But I am also a realist, and the reality is that this growth spurt we are in—hell that the whole economy is in—will wane at some point. Therefore, in addition to our course of action on bottom-line improvement and the eradication of waste, Susan and I are presenting to you today our strategic '5, 10, 20 Plans.'

"A 5, 10, 20 Plan is something I have created for my own business and something I believe we should be prepared here for at The Factory. In essence, 5, 10, 20 is a series of contingency plans we create in times of plenty to anticipate a slowdown in our business of 5%, 10%, and 20%. We create these plans in good times when there is no pressure on us from timelines and impending decisions. We created these strategic plans for The Factory over the last few days to give you an outline of our course of action, in the event we would need one. Think of these as our defensive playbooks.

"They are incomplete in all their tactics, but the strategy is clear, and over the following weeks we will be asking Steve, Tia, and other department leaders to create their own 5, 10, 20 Plans that will outline the steps they would take if tomorrow their budgets were cut by 5%, 10%, or 20%.

"Steve is also posting some job openings to add defensive players to our leadership team—people who specialize in efficiency, proficiency, and process. They will help us dig deeper, find more, and they will be 100% connected to the bottom-line.

"These plans and these people are crucial for the future survival of The Factory. Should we be faced with a downturn to our business, we can pull these plans from a drawer and get started on them.

"I personally have lived through two downturns myself, and in the first I lost my business. The second was very different because I was executing on my plan 20% reduction plan when my competitors were still trying to circle the wagons and get the Board together to talk about what was happening.

"Today we present to you the executive summaries of those plans in order for you to sign off on the strategy. This way, if something does happen, we have all already agreed to the course of action."

Ben sat down and looked around the room. The members were all looking through the plans in the back of the presentation and nodding.

"Damn good idea," was the consensus.

Susan stood. "Folks, let's take a break, get some lunch, and return. But before we vote on the new direction you have before you and the contingencies as Ben outlined, I want you to do something with me.

"Ben taught me a simple tool I use every day, twice a day; once when I arrive in the morning and a second time after I return from lunch. That tool and the exercise associated with it is so important I would not want to miss it for a single day, not even for you sitting here in this room. So therefore, before we move to a vote, I want to take you all on a Walkabout of our facility. I want you to respect the work being done, but ask questions, look at things, pick them up, touch them. Get in the dumpster if you must, but truly take time to see what it is we do here. I think you will be surprised. I know I was."

Notes from a Lean Manager's Playbook

The Fishbowl A leaky fishbowl cannot be resolved by adding water or replacing fish. It can only be resolved by repairing the leaks in the bowl. Modern management approaches the fishbowl problem by insisting that more revenue and upgraded or better-trained employees are the solution, even when logic tells us that only rational solution is to focus on fixing the bowl.

The Huddle is covered in the <u>Frontline Manager's Playbook</u> and is simplified for Frontline Managers in <u>Be A Frontline HERO</u>. The Huddle is a brief standup meeting that is done at least once each day. The objective is to talk about success, set goals for the day and uncover barriers in the process.

The employees should do 95% or more of the talking. The manager is just there to facilitate and find problems they need to address.

The Walkabout Every manager, without exception should walk the floor where the work is being done AT LEAST twice each day. The point of the walk is to be present, to show the team that you are paying attention, and to inspect the work being done. The Walkabout is NEVER confrontational; it is for information gathering, using the senses of the manager to walk around, develop relationships, and ask questions.

People will only respect what you inspect.

The Enemies of EBITDA These are the eight areas in every business where waste is found. Transportation, Inventory, Motion, Waiting, Over-production, Over-processing, Defects, and Skills. These will be the focus of this book, but there are three other areas that the author also considers enemies.

First, the enemy of Asymmetry; a business that does not have a consist flow of business or materials both in and out of the business. Seasonality, end-of-the-month order rushes, etc. all make a business asymmetrical, and asymmetrical businesses tend to struggle with wages and cost overruns.

Second, the enemy of Deviation; deviation is when the people in a company are not following a process and creating extra steps. Even if well-meaning, unchecked deviation can wreak havoc on a company. An extra, undocumented step creates an environment where scale is impossible because the people doing the jobs are the only ones that know the steps of the process. Furthermore, those extra steps or deviations may not be beneficial in light of the entire process. Any change to process requires insight and thought about the outcomes that change effects.

Last, the enemy of Excess Capacity. Do elements of your business only generate revenue when you are there actively working in or on them? Or do meeting rooms, machines, etc., sit empty at any time throughout the day and night? If so, then consider the creative ways you can use those spaces and equipment to increase your business.

The 5 Why's Most managers see a problem and try to solve it. The purpose of the 5 Why's is to stop that from happening and focus instead on why the problem started in the first place, asking "Why?" over and over about the problem until you expose its root cause. By solving the root cause, you resolve the problem permanently.

Just in Time Inventory Holding onto old inventory or raw materials is almost always a bad idea. Having on hand what is needed for that week, day or, ideally, shift is the optimal way to save space and money. Inventory of any sort costs money, be it real raw materials or items you just never got around to purging, liquidating or, in the case of businesses that write code, deleting or archiving.

As with a computer, the more stuff you keep on it the slower the machine runs. The same is true of every business. Don't fall into the idea of sunk costs. If a material, product, or file no longer brings value, get rid of it.

Process Mapping/Spaghetti Diagrams Motion and transportation can kill a company. Motion is the little things we do in our workspace while adding value. Things such as bending, turning, or running to the printer. These things add up, and many occurrences result in repetitive stress and overuse injuries. They contribute to waste because, when people aren't feeling there best—when they are tired, sore, or injured—their rate of work slows down, or they avoid doing critical tasks because of their pain. Optimizing workspaces produces better outcomes.

Transportation can be both internal and external. You must combat both. External logistics can often be resolved by having a tighter review process on costs, better negotiations, or thinking about why you do things the way you do. Combining shipment, having pickup windows, only shipping on certain days of the week, etc., can all help reduce costs and improve margins.

Internal Transportation, i.e., the steps people take to complete the work, is from our perspective the area where manufacturing companies need the most help. The feeding of lines, the movement of materials, and the access to inventory can and usually does translate into thousands of hours of wasted steps.

Diagramming, mapping, and process analysis are great tools to combat these enemies.

The Block, Tackle, or Handoff

Any time you face a new task, you must ask yourself three questions:

1. Can I handle this in my blocks?
2. Must I tackle this right now?
3. Can I hand this task off and delegate someone to handle it?

Setting apart time to get things done is the best way to control time.

1% Better Every day Most of us in management are programmed to look for big ideas. Innovation is expensive. What isn't expensive is incremental improvement. Challenge your team and your people to be better than yesterday, challenge the status quo, seek out improvement, and be thinking through the lenses of, "Can we automate this, could we outsource it, could we abbreviate the process, or could we eliminate this all together?" When Ben and Susan spoke about the 1035B's, Ben saw the opportunity to partner with The Shop because he was processing how eliminating the product might work. He then found that outsourcing it was a win-win for all parties.

A journey of 1,000 miles begins with one step. Take one and the miles will add up quickly.

Ohno Many times a process reaches a point where we believe it cannot be improved further. In those instances, and after we have trained our managers and people in the tools outlined in this book, we can then begin the process of removing resources.

Sometimes we are stuck because we can't believe something is possible. Being faced with a limitation on resources is a great way to break through that thinking. It is also part of a defensive approach to business to always know what can be done under stress and pressure.

We aren't suggesting cutting every process to the bone and putting stress and pressure on people and machines. On the contrary, knowing what is possible under pressure allows us as leaders to know the minimal amount of resources needed, and in times of trouble we know the limitations of our systems.

Few Minutes Many people say that the most expensive words in business are "we have always done it that way." Arguably, a close second is "it only takes a few extra minutes."

Minutes add up to hours, hours add up to weeks and, all of a sudden, we are paying for tens of thousands of minutes and hours in our Cost of Labor as well as waiting, over-processing, and delays in providing services to customers.

Hearing an employee utter "it just takes a few extra minutes" should send a frigid chill down the spine of every manager. That phrase is the sound of a river of profits being lost.

Sunk Costs Doubling down on a bad strategy, idea, product, or service isn't doing anyone favors. Gaining an outside perspective is often the only way to break yourself of this habit. One other way is to predetermine what metric you will use at a later date to gauge success or failure, and create a plan to deal with the failure.

For instance, "We will sell 10,000 of these new units next quarter or we will no longer manufacturer them. If that occurs, all remaining inventory will be liquidated in 30 days and then discarded."

Many managers and product people struggle with sunk costs. No one likes to admit failure and, in some companies, failure can be an inhibitor to promotion. Creating a fail-safe as part of the initial product plan is a quick and easy way to rid yourself of Sunk Cost challenges.

Sunk Cost challenges apply to product companies, but even more so to software and services, trying to put Band-Aids on bullet holes when all the while starting over and abandoning the current path or strategy is the most cost-efficient solution.

Change what they see Changing culture, awakening people and getting them to see that the business is changing actually requires more than just vision. It literally requires them to physically see something different.

Nothing changes the culture as fast as a coat of paint. There is something transformative about color; it makes people physically see that something is different. Moving furniture, machines, workspaces work well too. But nothing, I mean nothing, does more than a coat of paint.

Defense In every game, there are both offensive and defensive players. You must have both on your team to win. Yet, in business, the idea of defensive players is foreign. Sales, marketing, human resources, etc. are all working on growing revenue, improving or hiring better people, creating new products and services. Defense seems lost in the shuffle. But without it, profits are in jeopardy and, when outside forces like rising wages, tariffs, taxes or an economic slowdown occur, fully-offensive businesses disappear.

Challenge yourself and your team to hire some defensive talent on your team. Train your people in the methods of defense. Teach them that enemies abound, and it is up to them to stop them.

Epilogue

I hope you enjoyed reading this book as much as I enjoyed writing it.

Although a fictional story, the references, situations, and solutions were all ones taken from my real-life consulting work. If you are a client and think something sounded familiar, you are probably right. I thank you for the experience and am happy your story can help others.

Where The Frontline Playbook was focused on the AMP Tools, this book both adds to the tool set and also acts as a place to tell the stories of how our work, works!

I hope that you came away with nuggets of information, ideas, and tools that will improve your business. Moreover, I hope you embrace the last takeaway from this book to heart.

Having a 5, 10, 20 Plan in your drawer is a sure-fire way to survive changing market conditions. The future is unclear but planning today for what might happen tomorrow is a must.

Finally, if you would like to learn more about AMP, its tools, methods and additional resources, you can check out www.ampyouroutcome.com and find links to our books, content, and weekly office hours to ask questions and receive answers live.

Derrick & The AMP Team
info@ampyouroutcome.com

www.ingramcontent.com/pod-product-compliance
Lightning Source LLC
Chambersburg PA
CBHW072138170526
45158CB00004BA/1426